STEICHEN

BLUMENFELD

TIFFANY IN FASHION

John Loring

Essays by
Eleanor Lambert
and
James Galanos

HARRY N. ABRAMS, INC., PUBLISHERS

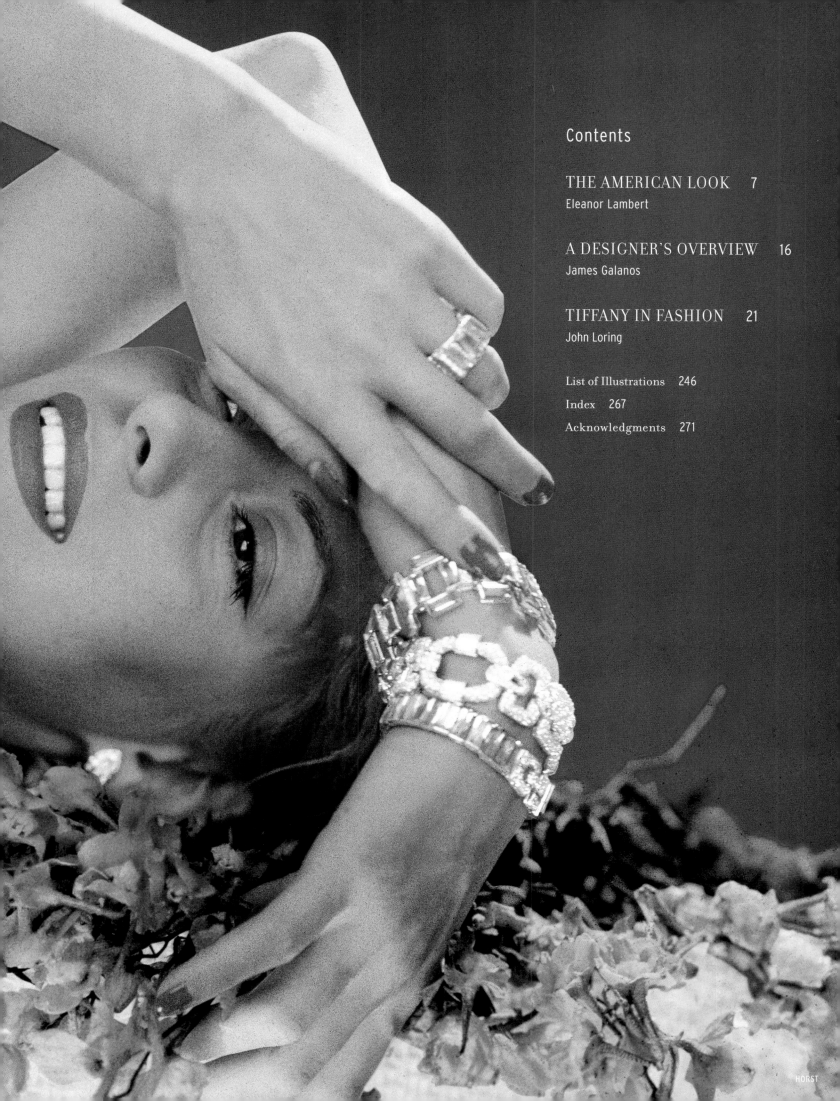

Contents

HORST

STEICHEN

THE AMERICAN LOOK

by Eleanor Lambert

*Fashion is a dictatorship by a succession of designers,
each with a "vision" of a different silhouette that
compels consumers to follow a "look."*

In the late eighteenth century, Rose Bertin (1747–1813), Marie-Antoinette's court dressmaker, was the first to make Paris fashion popular and important, and later, in the mid-nineteenth century, English draper Charles Worth (1825–1895) established himself in both London and Paris as "fashion's first dictator." Worth introduced the hoopskirt and crinoline, and designed for both Queen Victoria and France's style-setting and beautiful young Empress Eugénie, thus becoming the first fashion designer to affect every aspect of style on both sides of the Atlantic.

In 1924, Gabrielle Chanel made little silk dresses and put them and striking hats on mannequins whom she then sent as a group to the Chantilly racetrack. Chanel caused a fashion sensation, forever ending Worth's era of corsets and overstuffed furbelows and bringing fashion into modern times.

Gabrielle Chanel, along with Madeleine Vionnet (a true fashion great and the inventor of the revolutionary bias cut), Mainbocher, the often eccentric Elsa Schiaparelli, Jeanne Lanvin, Jean Patou, Augustabernard, and Robert Piguet, was among the first favorites of American fashion magazine photographers and editors.

The art of fashion photography was itself born only three years after Chanel's "little black dress," and its leading exponents Edward Steichen, George Hoyningen-Huene, Horst P. Horst, Cecil Beaton, George Platt Lynes, and art director Alexey Brodovitch, and the ever-inspiring fashion editors Edna Woolman Chase, Carmel Snow, Diana Vreeland, and Bettina Ballard began to present jewelry in fashion photography as the ultimate fashion accessory.

Jewelry had, of course, existed for centuries as a symbol of wealth rather than of style; but this all changed with twentieth-century designers such as Tiffany's Jean Schlumberger, who first designed jewelry for Elsa Schiaparelli, and later with Tiffany's Elsa Peretti, who had previously designed jewelry for Halston, and more recently with Tiffany's Paloma Picasso, who had designed jewelry for Yves Saint Laurent. They joined forces with fashion and created a totally stylish and modern design vocabulary for jewels and made jewelry an integral part of fashion.

Carmel Snow after leaving *Vogue* and becoming editor at *Harper's Bazaar* in 1933 soon proclaimed "the glitter of important jewels" a vital element of fashion. Edna Woolman Chase followed up at *Vogue* in announcing that "jewel pieces will be huge and affluent. The road . . . is paved with huge and humorous jewels."

The inventor of fashion photography, Edward Steichen, was the one who persuaded Tiffany & Co. to lend assorted armloads of diamond, ruby, emerald, and sapphire bracelets for the first Tiffany-jeweled formal fashion photographs for *Vogue* in 1933. In line with *Vogue*'s (and *Harper's Bazaar*'s) favoritism toward Paris haute couture in the 1930s, the models wore gowns by Chanel, Mainbocher, and Augustabernard.

The publication of such extraordinary fashion photography in magazines whose mission was to specifically guide the general public (or the wealthier portion thereof) in its wardrobe selection encouraged socially prominent ladies to take a less stiff-necked attitude toward the fashion press, with the result that they would meet with editors like Carmel Snow, Diana Vreeland, and Edna Woolman Chase, with her Broadway actress/writer daughter Ilka, on a social as well as a professional level. The fashion photographers moved freely at parties, cameras in hand, so that "what they wore" became an influential and familiar field of photojournalism with a broad following.

American fashion began to assert its independence from Paris in 1938 when the impish and publicity-aware designer and author Elizabeth Hawes wrote an irreverent book called *Fashion is Spinach*, and Dorothy Shaver, then vice president of New York department store Lord & Taylor, filled the Fifth Avenue windows with the works of young American designers instead of Paris originals. Shaver advertised "The American Look." The phrase caught on worldwide and was used by the press when other American stores (at first reluctantly) followed suit. Bergdorf Goodman, Saks Fifth Avenue, Neiman Marcus in Texas, California's I. Magnin, and Marshall Field in Chicago began to buy and feature American designers and even began to seek publicity in *Vogue* and *Harper's Bazaar*, although editors of those magazines still concentrated their reports on Paris.

Shops like Jay Thorpe, Henri Bendel, Bergdorf Goodman, Bonwit Teller, and Milgrim in New York began the adventurous seasonal showings of private collections designed by their own staff, but they also made copies of Paris originals. Ohrbach's department store, in New York, held fashion shows sending two models out at once, one wearing the Paris original, the other its copy. The large stores still put

their own label, instead of the designer's, into the back of the garment. I remember Adam Gimbel, the head of Saks Fifth Avenue, saying to me, "Our name is all we need" when I sought his support for using the designers' names.

The 1940s proved to be a landmark decade for American fashion, with designers like Hattie Carnegie, Nettie Rosenstein, and Sophie Gimbel establishing their reputations firmly and with Paris fading out during the war years.

Wartime restrictions on fabrics and on everything else needed by American, French, and British forces caused a sharp change in the design and consumer consumption of clothes. The silhouette became streamlined, simple, and influenced by movie stars as well as by such opera divas as Rosa Ponselle and Lily Pons. The great Chicago-born star of Paris couture, Mainbocher, reestablished his exclusive business in New York and created both theater costumes and private couture, with costumes for *One Touch of Venus* for actress Mary Martin and dresses for socialites Princess Natalie Paley and Mrs. Winston ("CZ") Guest, who were among his most visible clients. With wartime fabric restrictions, plus the shortages of all supplies needed by the armed forces, fashion supplies were scarce, but Mainbocher managed to open and maintain a salon in New York that kept his international clients happy and brought new fashion icons to world renown.

Other forces in the New York fashion world included Vienna-born couturier Hattie Carnegie, who had borrowed her professional name to create a more important impression, began as a milliner in 1909, introduced a full fashion collection in 1918, then went on to establish her own line of ready-to-wear made in her own factory just ten years later. The "little Carnegie suit," her best-known creation, was considered a status symbol during the 1930s, 1940s, and 1950s. In its October 1936 issue, *Harper's Bazaar* touted "the important little suit" as "a godsent uniform," and Carnegie suits were worn by a wide circle of international celebrities who regarded Miss Carnegie as their unquestioned arbiter of taste. She inspired her early employees, however briefly, including Claire McCardell, Jean Louis, Norman Norell, and Gustave Tassell, and later Pauline Trigère and James Galanos—all of whom became famed designers on their own. She remained a force in America until her death in 1956.

In the 1920s the appearances in New York of La Chauve-Souris and Diaghilev's Ballets Russes, with Vaslav Nijinsky in *L'Après-midi d'un faune* and Tamara Karsavinas as "The Dying Swan," were sensations

HOYNINGEN-HUENE

STEICHEN

that brought to America not only these visiting stars but also two other talented Russians, fashion great Valentina and her husband, theater director George Schlee, who were to become powerful members of the growing American fashion elite. Valentina created exotic, timeless, bias-cut dresses with sometimes only one seam, softly coutured year-round suits, navy blue silk day dresses with large, capable-looking red silk crêpe aprons tied on at the waist that became a fad. (Valentina and Greta Garbo made an impression. I remember clearly today when they came to our home for dinner in 1938 dressed identically in this outfit.) Valentina became wildly popular as a theatrical designer not only for Garbo but also for other dramatic actresses such as Katharine Hepburn, Gloria Swanson, Judith Anderson, Katharine Cornell, and Lynn Fontanne.

The *New York Times* commented: "Valentina designs clothes that act before a word is spoken." Her comment "Mink is for football" became a fashion classic.

Nettie Rosenstein, who in 1931 opened one of the first American high-fashion ready-to-wear dress houses to be run under a designer's own name, was best known as a leading designer of the "little black dress" from the 1930s through the 1950s. She designed Mrs. Dwight D. Eisenhower's inaugural ball gown, and her company, Nettie Rosenstein, Inc., is credited with having helped make ready-made clothing a major American industry.

In 1937 Pauline Trigère, a Parisian of Russian origin, like many European talents came to America to avoid the Nazi threat. She became for more than half a century a highly creative designer of couture quality ready-to-wear fashions. A New York personality as well as one of the important names in American fashion, she is remembered for her passion for red and for her famous dictum: "When you feel blue, wear red!"

Claire McCardell in 1938 took the spotlight in American fashion history as an independent designer uninterested in Paris influences. Her inspiration came from the soft, early American feeling of unconstructed clothes to which she brought her own architectural, modern shaping. She quickly established herself as the American designer most closely identified with the term "The American Look." Her best-known creation, the "monastic" dress, became popular throughout the world because of its loose and bias cut. What's more, she was the first to use wool tweed for evening clothes.

Norman Norell, called the "dean of American fashion designers," was among the first to use couture techniques and provide couture quality in ready-made clothing. First employed by Charles Armour, Norell went on to join Hattie Carnegie's staff, where he designed glamorous originals for such notables as Gertrude Lawrence, Paulette Goddard, and Ina Claire. In 1941, Norell, with business partner Anthony Traina, formed the design and manufacturing firm of Traina-Norell, bringing a new dimension of luxurious simplicity to ready-made clothes. He received the first Coty American Fashion Critics' Annual Award for clothing design just one year later. I had established this award with New York's official greeter and 1939–40 World's Fair impresario Grover Whalen (then the chairman of Coty) to recognize American fashion. The Coty Awards evolved into today's Council of Fashion Designers of America awards.

Despite having the largest history of ready-to-wear production in the world, and the greatest number of professional fashion designers, the United States has always been somewhat introverted in claiming its place among the arts. Leaders such as Bill Blass, James Galanos, Geoffrey Beene, Arnold Scaasi, Oscar de la Renta, Halston, and other outstanding talents had to be patient before they were acknowledged by foreign markets. Our fashion designers were practically unknown, except in America, until the formation of the New York Dress Institute in 1940 and the successful press program, which would follow. A unique contract was made between the International Ladies Garment Workers Union and the Dress Manufacturers Association, where the two organizations would pay one-half of one percent of their income into a fund each year to promote American fashion. At first planned as an advertising campaign, trite slogans on billboards were quickly disapproved of by American fashion stores such as Saks Fifth Avenue, Lord & Taylor, Neiman Marcus in Texas, I. Magnin in California, and Marshall Field in Chicago (largely with women presidents at the time), all of whom suggested a change to a more fluid form of publicity and recom-

mended me to carry this change forward. In 1940 I inherited this dream account as press director of the institute (and later as director), and my responsibilities with it lasted for more than fifty years.

The condition that I felt was essential was for me to immediately identify the New York Dress Institute with an elite group of designers whose work was already known to the public as being of couture standing. Known as the Couture Group of the New York Dress Institute, they did not all belong to the same division of the I.L.G.W.U., but they were recognized as creative designers with the couture standing of those in Paris. These highly talented individuals included Hattie Carnegie, Claire McCardell, Valentina, Nettie Rosenstein, Adele Simpson, Pauline Trigère, Jane Derby, Sally Milgrim, Sophie Gimbel, Charles James, Clare Potter, Lilly Daché, Monte Sano, John Frederics, and Hollywood designers Adrian and Howard Greer. We began biannual National Press Week fashion shows in New York in January 1943 (when there were only fifty-three fashion editors in the United States). Years later in 1967 with the help of Senator Jacob Javits and ex-Senator Henry Cabot Lodge, we were sent by the U.S. State and Commerce Departments to put on American fashion shows in Moscow on two separate occasions and then traveled the world from London to Paris to Japan.

The famous Versailles fashion show of 1973, however, really put American fashion on the international map. It was a gala affair that began by accident during a conversation between Gerald and Florence van der Kemp and me around a swimming pool at La Fiorentina, the Riviera home of our friend Mary Lasker. Gerald was the curator of the Palais de Versailles, and he asked me to help him organize a fund-raiser to restore the palace bedroom of Rose Bertin's old patron, Marie-Antoinette.

I headed the American committee for the show, which took place in November of 1973 and was the first collaboration of talents between American and French couture designers. My goddaughter Liza Minnelli sang "New York, New York" in front of a huge sketch of the Eiffel Tower as an opener. The show's French presentation was by Yves Saint Laurent, the house of Christian Dior, Pierre Cardin, Hubert de Givenchy, and Emanuel Ungaro. The American show was directed by dancer, singer, film actress, and author of *Eloise* books (and Liza's other godmother) Kay Thompson. It featured designers Bill Blass, Anne Klein, Stephen Burrows, Oscar de la Renta, and Halston, and everyone loved it. Baroness Marie-Héléne de Rothschild, the "Queen of Paris Society," was chairman of the French Social Committee. It was stage-directed by the chief director of the Comédie Française, and the benefit raised $265,000 (a fortune thirty years ago) for restorations at the Château de Versailles.

At the time of the Versailles show, Halston had already become the star of New York designers. He had made the sack dress with pockets the "rich uniform" of a generation of young Americans, including Jacqueline Kennedy and other icons of society, the theater, and movies. Halston also introduced novelty fabrics such as Ultrasuede and was world-famous as the designer of the pillbox hat, which was first worn by Jacqueline Kennedy and immediately became the rage throughout the world.

From the 1930s on, fashion itself influenced the design of "big" jewelry. In the 1930s a pair of large, pavé diamond clips were worn on shoulder straps of evening gowns or the lapels of chic suits, and twin jewels and then oversized jewels after the Paris Exposition des Arts et Techniques of 1937 were the latest thing; but Halston was the first American fashion designer to welcome the idea of putting real jewelry in their seasonal fashion shows with sterling silver designs by his star fashion model Elsa Peretti.

Beginning with the arrival of Elsa Peretti at Tiffany's in 1974 and Paloma Picasso in 1980, the world of fashion jewelry had its own major-league designers. Elsa's big, architectural hoop earrings and simple circular bangles, "Equestrian" belt buckles, and "Bone" cuff bracelets were required accessories with the people who wore Halston dresses, like Liza Minnelli, and with fashion editors, like Carrie Donovan, and they are still the rage today, as are Paloma Picasso's signature gold X's, colorful headlight-sized gemstones, and chunky semiprecious stone or amber necklaces.

American fashion today is a democracy headed by many individuals who suggest rather than dictate—except when groups of teenagers decide for themselves on a certain cut of jeans or on a fashion accessory like Tiffany's sterling silver "Tag" bracelets.

The last benevolent fashion dictator, Yves Saint Laurent, is now retired. He introduced the tuxedo to women's fashion and in the 1960s found a new kind of inspiration in the street.

Valentino, the Roman designer, shows regularly in America and is still an expert in highly decorative and ultrafeminine dresses, but he does not try to change fashion.

Giorgio Armani, however, has led both women and men into the present era where the key word is "comfort"—ease and a sort of slouchy unconstructed yet shapely chic—with slung belts on full-legged trousers and square jackets.

Geoffrey Beene, the New York designer whose impeccable style often inspires an elegant client to depend on Beene alone for her entire wardrobe and whose inventive bias cuts are the wonderment of all who see them, is currently America's most acclaimed active designer, having received the 2002 National Design Award in the American Original category.

With his superbly cut and detailed clothes, James Galanos, the unquestioned leader of the school of California fashion until his recent retirement in 2001, maintained the American haute couture standards set by Mainbocher in the 1940s.

Zoran, Isabel Toledo, Ricky Owens, Betsy Johnson, and John Anthony are among the current designers with large followings, but the undoubted leaders of the New York group are Geoffrey Beene, Carolina Herrera, Donna Karan, Calvin Klein, Ralph Lauren, Oscar de la Renta, and Arnold Scaasi.

Most of those today are part of the "big business" world, too, being backed by financiers who make it possible for each one to have his or her own stores, advertisements, trunk shows, and international ready-to-wear empires. As much as to clothes, they lend themselves to accessories, home furnishings, fragrances, shoes, handbags, lingerie, and even cars. They have become brands.

Tiffany & Co., founded in 1837, is, as it has been since Jean Schlumberger's arrival there in 1956, the great home of American fashion's name designer jewelry with the unequaled designs not only of Schlumberger but also of Elsa Peretti and Paloma Picasso. Tiffany & Co. continues to be an American institution.

STEICHEN

MICHAEL HALSBAND

HOYNINGEN-HUENE

A DESIGNER'S OVERVIEW

by James Galanos

The face-off between the two fashion centers
of Paris and New York began in the 1940s.

New York in the 1940s had some very great fashion establishments, the foremost being Hattie Carnegie. Carnegie was petite, impeccably dressed, and a dynamo, and the first to have a fashion empire in New York that included couture and deluxe ready-to-wear. It also comprised fashion accessories, costume jewelry, perfume, and a large retail boutique featuring all of her products as well as European couture pieces and American designer clothes. My fashion moment started in 1942, and a few years later Hattie Carnegie would buy Galanos for her retail shop at 42 East Forty-ninth Street.

Carnegie's astuteness and instincts were remarkable. She employed both Norman Norell and Jean Louis, who later formed their own design houses, and Jean Louis became a famous name in the motion picture industry. His creations for Rita Hayworth, Marlene Dietrich, and Loretta Young among others, would be seen around the world and influence many designers in both American and French couture.

Other designers of international distinction were Valentina, who gowned some of the most elegant women in New York with designs of daring simplicity, and Mainbocher, who before World War

II exited Paris for New York to establish his couture house after having had a highly successful career in Paris for a decade.

New York had names such as Jessie Franklin Turner and Nettie Rosenstein, each with his or her own individual style; the great Charles James, designer extraordinaire; and Norman Norell, who opened his own business in deluxe ready-to-wear and was admired for his beautiful clothing. Others like Germain Monteil and Pauline Trigère arrived from Paris and became names of great importance. There were, in fact, many talented designers that made New York fashion highly visible and exciting in the 1940s.

On the other side of the ocean, great French couture of the 1920s and 1930s thrived, but World War II would change the dynamics of fashion the world over and bring about the closure of many of the most famous couture houses in Paris. The incomparable Madeleine Vionnet, Cristóbal Balenciaga, Robert Piguet (with whom I had spent two years in Paris as an apprentice), Elsa Schiaparelli, Gabrielle "Coco" Chanel, Mainbocher, and others of equal importance closed their ateliers, refusing to collaborate with the Germans. Others remained to keep artisans

AVEDON

and their crafts alive for the future. The face-off between the two fashion centers of Paris and New York began in the 1940s.

French fashion designers were aware of the American scene; after all, they shared many of the world's most elegant women as clients, women who crossed the Atlantic Ocean yearly to view the French collections, make purchases, and be fitted at the great couture houses. Although a growing number of these clients were being clothed by their American counterparts, French couturiers and French fashion continued to be the most influential in the world until the 1940s when the center shifted to New York from Paris, which had been cut off from the American market by the German occupation.

Hollywood, California, with its great film industry clearly had a major influence around the world with its famous designers such as Gilbert Adrian and Travis Banton, who during the 1930s and 1940s costumed glamorous movie stars such as Greta Garbo, Joan Crawford, Marlene Dietrich, and Rosalind Russell. American films and their fashions reached an audience far greater than any couturier could have and were highly acclaimed, studied, and copied. A few French couturiers even attempted to design for Hollywood. Both Chanel and Schiaparelli had their moment, but they preferred working in their own milieu. Hollywood, of course, continues to exert its influence, with other designers providing important creations for today's great stars.

After the war years, Paris regained its preeminence with the sensational 1947 opening of the house of Dior. Christian Dior became the world's most famous designer, creating the "New Look"; his death in 1957 was mourned around the world. Dior's protégé Yves Saint Laurent then continued to design for the house of Dior. It had been expected that he would make a huge success there, but instead Saint Laurent opened his own establishment under his own name and became the most popular and copied designer of his time. At that same moment in the early 1960s in Paris, the magnificent Balenciaga, truly the most elegant designer in the world, was creating styles and designs that set the standards other designers could only dream of. His influence on world fashion was tremendous from the 1930s until his retirement at the end of the 1960s. After Balenciaga the world saw a decline in elegance and the coming of some remarkable changes in the fashion firmament. The sudden "youthquake" shook the universe of couture and the establishment. The preeminence of haute couture collapsed. It did not relate to what was going on in the world. For most, elegance was out, and the blue jean seemed to rule the world.

American ingenuity and expertise, combined with casualness, simplicity in lifestyle, and a freedom seldom seen before in all aspects and attitudes, were the way to go.

The French, the Italians, and the English became partners with Americans in fashion. The policy of "open hands across the ocean" and the growth of a "one world" of increasing economic interconnections and swifter transportation and communications all resulted in fashion designers and fashion trends throughout the world influencing one another to a greater extent than ever before.

DERUJINSKY

TIFFANY IN FASHION

by John Loring

"For some astounding reason we have suddenly made up our minds to dress up." —Carmel Snow, 1935

The first formal fashion photographs accessorized with jewels from Tiffany & Co. appeared in the July 1, 1933, issue of *Vogue*. They were by Edward Steichen, who had invented modern fashion photography seven years earlier with a portrait study of actress, model, and fellow photographer Marion Morehouse wearing a Paris couture gown by Cheruit. Steichen's models in the Tiffany-jeweled photographs were young New York socialites; their summer evening gowns were predictably from Paris designers. Background décor was by the Tiffany of New York's interior design world of the 1930s, W. & J. Sloane; and each model wore a small fortune in Art Deco bracelets. These first black-and-white masterpieces combining Tiffany and fashion were followed in *Vogue*'s December 1, 1934, issue with an early full-color Steichen image, captioned "The Ultimate in Christmas Loveliness." In it a sophisticated European model wears an emerald-green crêpe dress by Paris couturier Yvonne Carette and "a snowy-white fox cape" from the ultimate Paris furrier Revillon.

At the depth of the Great Depression, the reasonably simple and probably reasonably inexpensive Carette cocktail dress was accessorized with $64,000 of emerald and diamond bracelets comple-

mented by a "snowy-white" sautoir of natural pearls for an additional $26,000, totaling a then-staggering $90,000 (staggering because at that time working Americans earned about $1,000 a year—and almost one out of four workers was unemployed).

In the Great Depression, the New York fashion press, like the Hollywood film industry, felt it was its duty as a young American institution to lift the spirits of the poverty-stricken United States with images of what photography historian John Kobal aptly described in 1976 in his fashion-conscious book *Hollywood Glamour Portraits* as "more unreachable splendor that outshone, outspent and outdid the old dreams of the old America."

Tiffany's had not accessorized the earliest fashion photographs or early Hollywood glamour photos, although there was no lack of jewelry in *Vogue* and *Harper's Bazaar* at the end of the 1920s and the outset of the 1930s. Early Hollywood star portraits such as Eugene Robert Richee's 1927 Paramount publicity shots of Olga Baclanova costumed by Howard Greer and his more famous 1928 portraits of Louise Brooks, as well as his photos the same year of Esther Ralston, show the three Paramount stars well jeweled, wearing long sautoirs of pearls and assorted gem-set ornaments, which, like the pearls

Audrey Hepburn wore thirty-three years later in *Breakfast at Tiffany's*, were in all likelihood from the costume department at Paramount.

There is a simple explanation for Tiffany's belated entry into the field of accessorizing fashion photographs seven years after Steichen's innovative shot of Marion Moorehouse: Louis Comfort Tiffany, son of Tiffany's founder and the greatest decorative artist America has produced, retained control over his company's image until his death on January 17, 1933, and with his profoundly turn-of-the-century Art Nouveau aesthetic, he had been diametrically opposed to the Art Deco style of late 1920s and early 1930s fashion photography.

Under Louis Comfort Tiffany's control from 1902 to 1933, Tiffany & Co. had remained a bastion of near-fanatic old-world conservatism. Its jewels were never photographed unless they were to be put on display at American world's fairs, such as St. Louis's Louisiana Purchase Exposition of 1904 or San Francisco's Panama-Pacific International Exposition of 1915, or at various Paris salons, and Tiffany's in no way agreed to join the modern world by including photographs in its advertising until the Great Depression drove the company to it in the spring of 1931 when, as the trade journal *Advertising & Selling* noted on June 24 (only eighteen months before Mr. Tiffany departed), "Advertising's last stronghold of chaste austerity has now been broached—henceforth Tiffany ads are to include photographs." On November 19, 1931, *Printer's Ink* added, "Bring the smelling salts! Tiffany & Company, ultra-ultra-conservative jewelers, have kicked over the traces and gone modern in their advertising. They are actually using pictures."

The inclusion of Tiffany jewels in fashion photography was obviously out of the question up until January of 1933. Moments later it was open to consideration, and George Heydt, then Tiffany's advertising manager, saw its possibilities. He was, even during the Great Depression, spending a small fortune of Tiffany's monies advertising in *Harper's Bazaar*, *Vogue*, *Town & Country*, and *Vanity Fair*. Further publicizing Tiffany's jewels by lending them to photo shoots at these magazines could not really be interpreted as "a compromise with greedy commercialism," as stodgy trade publications had labeled the first appearances of photography Heydt had authorized in Tiffany ads.

He did it, but he was not willing to discuss it. Heydt noted in a signed letter of December 7, 1935, preserved in the Tiffany Archives, that a reporter from *Women's Wear Daily* had asked for an interview to "discuss our new policy of publicity."

"I replied that we were not ready to discuss publicity at the present time, but that if he would call up after the holidays we would take the matter under consideration."

It appears that the Tiffany advertising and publicity department had taken the matter under consideration a month or so after Louis Comfort Tiffany was no longer in the background to supervise them, since Tiffany jewels appear in photo essays on the lifestyles of prominent young socialites by the late spring and early summer of 1933 in both *Vogue* and *Harper's Bazaar*. The model for *Harper's Bazaar*'s June 1933 double-page society/fashion reportage accessorized by stacks of Tiffany diamond bracelets was no less a personage than Princess Xenia of Russia (a cousin of the unfortunate Czar Nicholas II) who had reinvented herself as a celebrity of New York society. The January 1934 issue of *Harper's Bazaar* followed up with a four-page photo essay by one of the first and most noted woman commercial and society photographers, the German aristocrat Baroness Toni von Horn, who was a friend and protégée of German-born Wall Street banking czar and philanthropist Otto Kahn. Toni von Horn's photo essay featured "Four Evenings in the Life" of Washington, D.C., Newport, and New York socialite Mrs. Allan Ryan, Jr., who, not at all coincidentally, was closely related by marriage to Otto Kahn's daughter Mrs. John Barry ("Nin") Ryan, Jr. (The Ryan ladies' husbands were first cousins and equal heirs to their grandfather Thomas Fortune Ryan's considerable estate.)

These 1933 and early 1934 *Vogue* and *Harper's Bazaar* photos accessorized with Tiffany jewels are stylish society portraits of the very rich or very titled much in the manner of Hollywood glamour portraits of Greta Garbo, Jean Harlow, Norma Shearer, and Joan Crawford at MGM, or of Paramount's portraits of Carole Lombard and Marlene Dietrich. They were not true fashion photographs.

The line between 1930s fashion photography and 1930s Hollywood glamour portraits is difficult to draw for two basic reasons. First, because New York's fashion photographers frequently used actresses as models as they do today; however, in the 1930s they were seldom stars (unless, like Katharine Hepburn, they appeared on Broadway) but instead were minor young actresses such as Steichen's favorite Danish-born Gwili André, whose often stunning successes were in the pages of *Vogue* with Steichen and other photographers and whose Hollywood ventures with David O. Selznick at RKO are best forgotten. Second, because Hollywood's costume designers—like Adrian at MGM, who dressed Jean Harlow, Norma Shearer, Joan Crawford, and Greta Garbo for both their films and glamour portraits—had legitimate claims to the title of "fashion designer," and Hollywood's costume designers did exert an important influence on American fashion in New York.

There was, as *Vogue* stated the case in its February 1, 1938, issue, that other inciter of burning feminine dress ambitions—the moving picture:

> *Constantly flickering before every child, girl, and woman in the U.S.A. is filmdom's languorous and unreal elegance, filmdom's philosophy that the road to happiness is via a glamorous gown, the symbol of life's success an ermine coat. Whatever else Hollywood may be, it certainly is the most perfect visual medium of fashion propaganda that ever existed.* (p. 153)

As for America's fashion photography, it should be noted that the Hollywood photo style, probably nowhere better exemplified than by Josef von Sternberg's lighting of Marlene Dietrich in her 1932 publicity shots for *Shanghai Express*, did not go unnoticed by New York art directors and photographers.

Tiffany & Co. entered the field of accessorizing fashion photography at the opportune time when the legendary mother of all American fashion editors, Edna Woolman Chase at *Vogue*, put her considerable power behind promoting extravagant showings of jewels to lift depressed mid-Depression spirits. The December 1, 1934, issue of *Vogue*, which featured Steichen's color photo of his model sporting $90,000 of Tiffany jewels, offered this editorial advice on holiday shopping:

FOR WIVES OR GRAND PASSIONS: JEWELS.
Husbands do not have to be told that nothing equals jewellery for restoring the lost gilt of romance in marital relations. There's something illicit about jewels, and wives adore illicit presents. It makes them feel like movie mistresses. (p. 62)

This interest in jewels and the tip of the hat to Hollywood influences were quite a departure for the generally conservative Chase. Although the Steichen cover of her December 1 issue of the previous year showed an ermine-clad model profusely jeweled with a diamond tiara, large emerald-cut diamond ring, and pendant earrings, there were no cover credits beyond "Cover design—color photograph by Steichen," and jewelry was quite absent in the editorial except for Tiffany's first full-page color still-

life of jewels to appear in a fashion magazine. (The photo was by Anton Bruehl.) The caption read only "J is for jewels"; the descriptions appeared tucked in at the back of the book on page 96 with the rather facetious lead line: "Now we come to the joolry [*sic*], the really elegant stuff picked out regardless." More realistic gift suggestions appeared in the "Fashions" section under "*Vogue*'s smart economies."

As for fashion in the December 1, 1934, *Vogue*, Broadway's—if not Hollywood's—influence, and with it the influence of American designers, began to emerge.

Edna Woolman Chase could not ignore Hollywood, but she was closer to and more focused on Broadway for the very basic reasons that she was a New Yorker and her beautiful young daughter Ilka was a Broadway actress. Her December 1 issue included the feature "Spotlight on Stage Clothes" by Marya Mannes (pp. 80–81) illustrated with photographs of two actresses gowned by Chicago-born, New York fashion maverick Elizabeth Hawes; along with Judith Anderson and Hedda Hopper gowned by Sophie (Gimbel) of Saks Fifth Avenue; and inevitably her daughter Ilka Chase in a dress by the Vienna-born empress of New York fashion design, Hattie Carnegie. The existence of Paris couture was acknowledged only by Tallulah Bankhead in a Schiaparelli gown.

Tiffany jewelry, once on the fashion pages in the mid-1930s, was there to stay, and Tiffany jewelry design evolved with American fashion design, if not totally hand-in-hand, on parallel paths as it progressed to the prevailing situation today that sees Tiffany & Co. as the only great internationally known jeweler that features name designers of high-fashion jewelry—Jean Schlumberger, Elsa Peretti, and Paloma Picasso.

From 1904 until 1933, all Tiffany & Co.'s "designer" jewelry was the creation of Louis Comfort Tiffany and designers who worked under his direction, principally Julia Munson from 1904 to 1914 and then Meta Overbeck from 1914 to 1933. Their designs were colorful and innovative, and some were masterpieces that could be looked at in their strong coloring and often bold scale and in their mixture of precious and not-at-all-precious materials as legitimate predecessors of designer fashion jewelry. However, Louis Comfort Tiffany's refusal to allow this quite extensive line of Tiffany "art jewelry" (as he called it) to be publicized in fashion magazines kept it in relative obscurity and allowed for only limited production and distribution.

E. R. RICHEE

E. R. RICHEE

Ironically, *Town & Country* published a full-page photo of Tiffany jewels in its December 1935, issue that featured a large Louis Comfort Tiffany/Meta Overbeck bracelet of circa 1930 and necklace of superb green tourmaline cabochons from Maine, with both bracelet and necklace worn on the model's arm, but there was no mention of Louis Comfort Tiffany. The heading read "Gems Circa 1935." The text stated that "The smooth despotism of the modern girl has had a chaste influence on all design. She is a completely stylized decoration herself, from her sculpted curls to the Artemis-austerity of her dinner gown. She demands the same ruthless simplification from her architect, her dressmaker and her jeweler. The photographs illustrate Tiffany & Company's response to the young idea." Louis Comfort Tiffany would have been astonished to learn that "the smooth despotism" of the young and fashion-conscious had had a "chaste influence" on his opulent designs five years after the fact.

"Ruthless simplification" had not been the theme of fashion or the fashion press in the late 1920s nor during most of the 1930s. In fact it was exquisitely detailed Paris haute couture from Worth, Chanel, Lanvin, Schiaparelli, Vionnet, Rouff, Mainbocher, Molyneux, Augustabernard, Patou et al. that had filled the pages of *Vogue* and *Harper's Bazaar*, whereas American fashion houses such as Hattie Carnegie, Milgrim, Jay Thorpe, Henri Bendel, Bergdorf Goodman, Saks, and Bonwit Teller in New York, I. Magnin in Los Angeles, and Martha Weathered in Chicago, and so forth did very little more than import, copy, or adapt Paris couture styles.

Tiffany & Co. had its Louis Comfort Tiffany designer jewelry line, but its core business of diamond, ruby, emerald, sapphire, and pearl jewelry was totally—like American fashion—under the influence of Paris and Tiffany's Paris branch, whose design staff stuck to the omnipresent French Art Deco style of the time.

Not all 1935 fashion commentators agreed with *Town & Country* on "simplification." *Harper's Bazaar*'s November 1935 issue's opening editorial observations called out for "Gowns of silver lamé. Bright, bright red crêpe. Belts blazing like Thaïs. The glitter of important jewels. Gold flowers in the hair. This is a season for great dash and dare. A new momentum has captured America. For some astounding reason we have suddenly made up our minds to dress up" (p. 49).

As the Great Depression continued into the second half of the 1930s, fashion and jewelry design did begin to modernize and somewhat simplify, if not

TONI VON HORN

yet Americanize. By 1936, Carmel Snow, the editor of *Harper's Bazaar* and "the Irish-accented voice of fashion authority" (as the *New York Times* called her) announced:

> The most important news from Paris is the dinner dress. It is totally fresh in conception. Its color is probably black. It has the muted elegance of perfection.
>
> Your dress may be black, but your kid shoes are a strong vital color . . . your jewelry, too, must be strong and colorful, mostly gold. (*Harper's Bazaar*, October 1936, p. 77)

Elaborately draped and detailed Paris gowns with stacks of Art Deco diamond, ruby, emerald, and sapphire bracelets were gradually on their way out, and a new kind of jewelry began to play a more and more important role in fashion and fashion photography, as did the simpler lines of American fashion designers.

Carmel Snow's former boss at *Vogue*, the even more conservative Edna Woolman Chase, subscribed to fashion's new gold standard a year later in her October 25, 1937 issue in a feature bluntly titled "Greed for Gold":

> Again, there's a great greed for gold—rich yellow gold and hoards of it. No little gram-weight nuggets content this age—your jewel pieces will be huge and affluent.
>
> There's a fine free attitude about jewels to-day—just as about clothes—the only law is to be profligate, personal, and entertaining.
>
> Around wrists—innumerable great gold bracelets.

The editor went on to note a new force in fashionable jewelry design, the young Frenchman Jean Schlumberger, an associate of Elsa Schiaparelli and one of the founding fathers of fashion jewelry, who would later play a central role at Tiffany & Co.

> The Duchess of Kent bought from that new designer in Paris, Jean Schlumberger, beautiful gold flying-fish earrings with diamond fins—so large they half cover the ear. Earrings have never been more entertaining.
>
> Nothing strikes such a false note in this day and age as dinky, small fry jewels. The real thing . . . is enormous, entertaining, ornamental, personal and witty.
>
> Have, if precious stones are beyond you, massive gold bracelets and clips. The road to glitter in 1937

is paved with huge and humorous jewels. (pp. 75 and 77)

"The road to glitter" led directly to the Paris Exposition des Arts et Techniques of 1937 where considerable importance was given to large-scale jewels, especially those with flower motifs. The trend was dictated to America by the great fashion guru of *Harper's Bazaar*, Diana Vreeland, in one of her witty and influential "Why don't you—?" features:

> FOR TOWN THIS WINTER—
> Chanel's waistcoat of black suede with black wool knit sleeves and all your jewels pulled out on top.
> Jewelry—
> Wear a blue sapphire thistle in one ear and a ruby thistle in the other. On each lapel pin a larger thistle, the color reversed.
>
> Appear with all the jewels on your left side, diamonds set in platinum . . . and on your right side, duplications of these ornaments only without the diamonds and in plain gold.
>
> Have the most beautiful necklace in the world made of huge pink spiky coral with big Siberian emeralds. Wear, like the Duchess of Kent, three enormous diamond stars arranged in your hair in front.
>
> Wear yellow diamond flowers in your ears, a flower clipped to the lobe of one ear, another flower clipped to the top of the other.
>
> Remember that long swinging diamond chandelier earrings are frightfully smart again, and wear them occasionally as Madame Sert does, pinned four inches below either shoulder on a high-necked black satin dress.
>
> Consider the chic of wearing bracelets high on the arm and try Lady Mendl's thin black leather bracelets which she wears just above the elbow with a huge diamond bracelet at the wrists. (*Harper's Bazaar*, November 1937, p. 113)

The message was heard by any and all conscious of fashion, including Tiffany's designers, who were already at work on jewels to be shown at New York's answer to the Paris Exposition des Arts et Techniques of 1937, the New York World's Fair of 1939–40.

Their designs for Tiffany's astounding display in the fair's House of Jewels featured a lavish tiara of emerald-centered diamond flowers with a 75-carat square-cut emerald, once the property of Sultan Abdul Hamid II of Turkey, at its center. There was also a great diamond and ruby "comet" brooch honoring the advent of the aerodynamic age and a ruby and diamond orchid brooch big enough to satisfy the

TONI VON HORN

most immodest fancies of Diana Vreeland herself. A cascade of 429 diamonds holding a 217½-carat aquamarine formed a showstopper necklace, and there were ample "huge diamond bracelets," one remarkable for a rare and also huge emerald-cut pink beryl at its center. All these jewels soon appeared in Edward Steichen fashion photographs in the pages of *Vogue*, some in the October 15, 1939, issue and the rest in the October 15, 1940, issue.

According to the 1939 accompanying article in *Vogue*, entitled "The Inimitable":

The fake can be fun, the synthetic can put up a nice show, but still eyes turn un-swervingly to the real thing in jewels. The pseudo is never quite as soul-satisfying. The lapel under the paste pin has never

quite the same unalloyed lift as the one under the precious clip. Perhaps, too, in these times of uncertainty, eyes turn to bona-fide jewels for their very certainty—for their tangible beauty in a world of all too little beauty; for their tangible value in a world of all too many teetering values.

Significant among the new jewel trends is a sud-den blaze for white stones: the cold white fire of diamonds.

Significant, too . . . A new partiality for platinum—the supply of which is becoming scarcer and scarcer now that it is being conscripted for the manufacture of high explosives. A new acquisitiveness for "sets" of jewels—necklace, clip, bracelet, ring all as deliberately matched up as a Victorian parlour set. A growing ennui for armfuls of junky

ANTON BRUEHL

jangles and bangles, and a new appreciation for one dramatic, self-sufficient bracelet . . . one factor remains constant—the personal, the inimitable. This may be the year of Ersatz in many things—but not in jewels. (p. 40)

World War II changed every aspect of American culture, and its ominous beginnings demanded change in both fashion and jewelry design. As the German army marched on Paris, America was about to be cut off from the source of so much of its fashion and design inspiration and, turning to itself, Americanized both, bringing American style into focus.

Vogue again stated the case clearly at the beginning of 1940 in its February 1 issue:

AMERICAN STYLE
Fashions with a National Accent,
Native or Naturalized
It is no news that American clothes to-day have a definite and recognizable quality of their own. Sometimes, they achieved this by purely American design; sometimes by the intelligent adaptation, evolution, or naturalization of French designs. But . . . in their own field they have a quality recognized all over the world of fashion.

What is news is the stirring life in the creative field of American clothes; an excitement, a cry for recognition, a wish for a real excellence that shall be our very own. We are newly eager to stamp every expression of our lives "American." . . . [I]n the new creative urge, the intelligent American designer freely admits his debt to France—while he is working steadfastly to produce something that shall be entirely his.

There has come to be a quality which, if not entirely native in source, is surely American in result. American fashion is something which blends and fuses the wit and subtlety of the French; the reticent elegance of the Spanish; the uncompromising straightforwardness of the English; the dark femininity of the Italian, into a new thing—American style. (p. 86)

This was reinforced in the October 15, 1940, issue of *Vogue* in a feature by Allene Talmey on New York fashion heralding "A torch-light parade of Americanism":

New York now is a city of beauty and interminable war talk . . . the shops have beautiful clothes, this time not from the French Collections, but solely from the brains and fingers of America.

Into the vacuum left by the lack of French clothes rushed the American designers. With great hoop-la, the newspapers interviewed, reviewed, and photographed them as though they were chorus-girls. With equal hoop-la, three of the houses had evening Openings of their first completely American fashions.

At Bergdorf Goodman's, Mr. Goodman, tall, silvery-haired, distinguished, and a little worried, stage-directed everything, reminding the girls to remove their jackets, to swirl their skirts. And then, at the end, after a toast to the French and the American couture, he brought on the house's seven designers, all embarrassed and pleased.

At Hattie Carnegie's, with Miss Carnegie behind the scenes, there were music, champagne, and even more photographers, most of them concentrating at one point on two figures dressed alike in hypnotic-red jersey.

At Saks-Fifth Avenue, the photographers, however, concentrated on Mayor LaGuardia, who fussed [over] the models and amused the crowd. But in the midst of all the goings-on, the gags, and the champagne, the speeches by the Mayor and by Adam Gimbel, the appearance of designers, Sophie Gimbel and Emmett Joyce, the clothes—fresh, cleverly simple, and for evening romantically beautiful—were taken seriously by both Saks and the audience.

Through all the Collections, there were beauty, and drama, and showmanship, and, above all, a passionate but discriminatory feeling for the American designers—all three million of them. (p. 40)

Beginning in its September 1, 1940, issue, *Harper's Bazaar* ran its own version of this with a two-volume "all-American fashion story":

This is the first issue of Harper's Bazaar that has ever appeared without fashions from Paris. We publish this record of the New York autumn openings with pride in the achievements of our American designers and with full acknowledgment of our debt to the French. We have learned from the greatest masters of fashion in the world; learned and then added something of our own. Such clothes have never been made in America before. (p. 44)

The September 15 issue continued:

We have splashed it with color. Forget your inhibitions and steep your mind in it—for color runs riot through the designs of the great made-to-order dressmakers of this country. You will find a choice of tweeds, the best made in America. Little dresses

STEICHEN

TONI VON HORN

TONI VON HORN

HOYNINGEN-HUENE

for movie nights. City-country woolens, picked with an eye to price. . . . (p. 35)

At first Tiffany's went along extending its collections of gold with gem-accent "American Deco" or "Retro Modern" jewels, all spirals and undulations and steps of gold combined with fluid snake chains, which it had begun in late 1935, looking forward to both the company's one-hundredth anniversary in 1937 and the New York World's Fair of 1939–40. Less expensive and clean-lined all-gold jewelry as well took on an importance in the Tiffany collections. And, for the first couple of years of the 1940s, both gold-with-gem-accent and all-gold Tiffany jewels along with the lavish diamond pieces unsold during the Great Depression continued to be loaned to fashion shoots.

This stopped at the end of 1942, as the war escalated and Tiffany's turned its attentions more toward manufacturing for the American military rather than developing new lines of jewelry. It would not be until eleven years later, in 1953, that Tiffany's again allowed any of its jewels to be photographed by the press, and then curiously only by *The Saturday Evening Post* for its January 31, 1953, issue.

Not until the fashion- and publicity-savvy chairman of Tiffany's neighbor on Fifth Avenue, Bonwit Teller's Walter Hoving, had bought control of the company from the Tiffany family in 1955 did Tiffany jewels reappear in fashion shoots for *Town & Country*, *Vogue*, and *Harper's Bazaar*. At first the jewels were high-end diamond pieces, an $81\frac{3}{4}$-carat diamond necklace photographed by Irving Penn for *Vogue*'s May 15, 1956, issue on a model wearing a Christian Dior–style cowl-collared green silk-chiffon overblouse; a floral diamond brooch modeled on a more American and quintessentially stylish James Galanos short linen evening dress shot by Gleb Derujinsky for *Town & Country*'s June 1956 issue; and long pendant diamond earrings photographed by Richard Avedon on his legendary model Dovima wearing two of the enduring American couturier Mainbocher's long, pale-colored crêpe evening dresses for *Harper's Bazaar*'s December 1956 issue.

In 1956, Walter Hoving brought the father of fashion jewelry design Jean Schlumberger to design for Tiffany & Co. introduced in *Town & Country*'s December 1956 issue in a stunning portrait of America's most widely celebrated society beauty, Mrs. Winston ("CZ") Guest, wearing a gray flannel Mainbocher dress and mink jacket, Schlumberger's chic and fanciful jewels from Tiffany's became a near

necessity in fashion photographs. They were shown
with the clothes of a broad range of America's top
designers, from James Galanos, Arnold Scaasi, and
Nettie Rosenstein to Philip Hulitar, Lilly Daché, and
Hannah Troy in the late 1950s; and on to more
Galanos and Mainbocher or Donald Brooks and Bill
Blass in the late 1960s; and so on until current times
where Schlumberger jewels have recently accessorized everything from a sensual satin Paris couture
dress by Emanuel Ungaro to a casual ready-to-wear
Byblos shirt worn with an Armani skirt.

Jean Schlumberger was the single greatest force
in the creation of fashion jewelry, a category that
was not—like fashion photography—born out of the
luxuries and glamour of an art-nurturing period of
boundless prosperity (the Roaring Twenties) but
rather out of the necessities of a period of great hard-
ship (the Great Depression of the thirties).

In jewelry, before Schlumberger there was a
choice between real precious stone and pearl jewelry
for those who could afford it—and many could in the
1920s—or paste copies for those who could not.

That all changed in the Great Depression. Of
course, there were stylish and now legendary social
ladies with still great fortunes such as the Duchess
of Kent (for whom Schlumberger made the oversized
flying-fish earrings remarked upon by Edna Woolman Chase at *Vogue* in 1937), Singer Sewing Machine
heiress Mrs. Reginald ("Daisy") Fellowes, American society's pet beauty Mrs. Harrison ("Mona")
Williams, and so forth who were all Schlumberger's
clients, but even for them the visually lavish jewels
he created often used more decorative than precious
materials. The Paris fashion world had need for a
totally new and affordable alternative to precious
gems, and Jean Schlumberger was the man with
the imagination, vision, wit, and stylishness to
answer them.

Recognizing his unique take on design, which
like her own had Surrealist leanings, Schiaparelli at
first asked him to make jewel-like buttons for her
clothes in 1937 ("Not one looked like what a button
was supposed to look like," Schiaparelli observed)
and then jewels for her circus-themed landmark
couture show of 1938.

Schlumberger responded with buttons and
jewels made out of chessmen, locks, miniature hand
mirrors, porcelain flowers plucked from chande-
liers, bright-colored enamels—"jewelry that [could]
afford to make fun of its own importance, suggest-
ing that the ultimate luxury may be a sense of
humor," as Holly Brubach so aptly wrote in the style
section of the *New York Times Magazine* (November

ANTON BRUEHL

5, 1995). Fashion at last had its own jewels, splen-
did, celebratory, and beautiful like fashion itself at
its best.

All this obviously had to come to a screeching
halt as World War II got under way. Schlumberger
joined the French army in 1939 and then Charles
de Gaulle's Free French Forces in 1942, where he
served through the end of the war and on into 1946.

The only continuation of the concept of fashion
jewelry during the war years that is remembered
today came from the imagination of the Chicago-
born designer Mainbocher, who had closed up shop
in Paris as the war began and reopened in New York.
The repatriated great of American fashion came up
with a new alternative to then unaffordable fine jewelry with his introduction of the decorated sweater
in 1941, which remained in style until the early to
mid-1950s. Continuing this idea of costume jewelry
as a built-in element of couture, he also at times
embroidered gold braid necklaces directly onto his
cocktail or evening dresses.

In 1946 Schlumberger moved to New York and
again began to design jewels. There nine years later
Walter Hoving asked him to join Tiffany & Co.

EMELIE DANIELSON

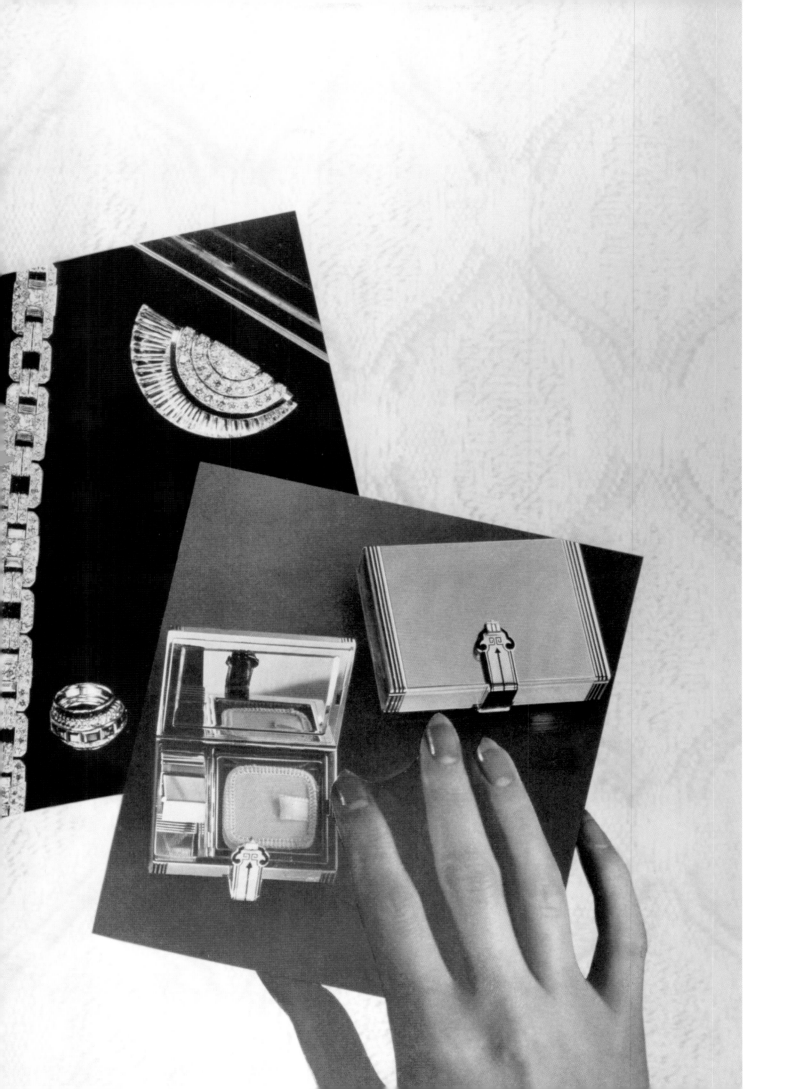

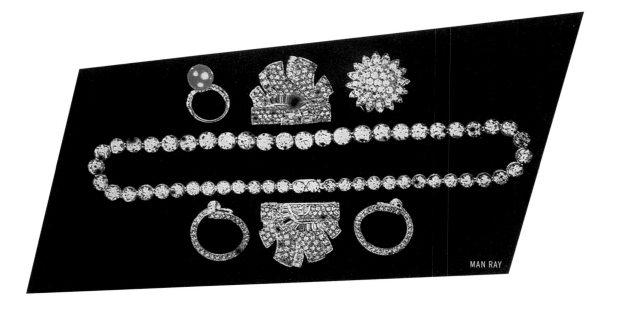

MAN RAY

In his Tiffany jewels, all the stylishness and imagination remained, but the vast resources of Tiffany's (and Walter Hoving's insistence on placing no restrictions on his designers) brought Schlumberger's jewelry designs to a new level.

"If we believe that certain jewels can be sheer poetry," Schlumberger put it, "this is more likely to be born of an unshackled discipline. Then, full of renewed hope, the creative spirit will blossom, totally expressive and totally itself."

Schlumberger's creative spirit blossomed at Tiffany & Co. into the most imaginative and stylish collections the world of jewelry and fashion had ever seen.

The jewels were generally based on the designer's love of the idiosyncratic aspects of nature's flora and fauna.

"I try to make everything look as if it were growing, uneven, at random, organic, in motion," Schlumberger explained. "I want to capture the irregularity of the universe."

"He so well understands the fantastic beauty of the world," Diana Vreeland added.

His clients included the most fashionable and socially prominent women in the world—Daisy Fellowes, Mona Williams (later Countess Mona von Bismarck), Gloria Guinness, Rachel "Bunny" Mellon, Pauline de Rothschild, Barbara "Babe" Paley, the Duchess of Kent, Diana Vreeland, Jacqueline

Kennedy, Carroll Petrie, and Françoise de la Renta— as well as film stars such as Jane Fonda and Elizabeth Taylor.

Fashion editors responded not only by accessorizing countless fashion shoots throughout the world with Schlumberger but by publishing full-page portraits of Schlumberger jewels as fashion statements in themselves, a genre of fashion photography originated by Hiro. The first jewelry-as-fashion Schlumberger study by Hiro appeared in the January 1960 issue of *Harper's Bazaar* with the caption "Sea-Trove: Schlumberger of Tiffany uses the precious jewels of the earth to recreate the fauna, rich and strange, of the underseas."

To this day the fashionable, rich, strange, and quintessentially elegant jewels of Jean Schlumberger continue to take their preeminent place in fashion photography nearly a half a century after their debut at Tiffany's.

Nine years after Schlumberger came to Tiffany's, a young American designer, Donald Claflin, joined Tiffany's, where he would create his own exotic menagerie of jeweled dragons, basilisks, reptiles, insects, and assorted children's storybook creatures as well as appropriately lavish jeweled flora to prop their post-Carrollian world. Claflin's were the perfect, gracefully flamboyant fairy-tale jewels to accessorize the intensely colorful fairy-tale fashions of the Swinging Sixties, as the Pop generation's decade

IVAN DMITRI

STEPHEN COLHOUN

is known, a decade when high fashion frequently found its inspirations in the both studied and eccentric youth culture styles of London's Carnaby Street and King's Road.

Claflin's extravagant Tiffany jewels were so visually assertive that they tended to take the spotlight away from clothes in fashion photography, which led the ever keenly observant Diana Vreeland to pose a memorable Donald Claflin fashion photograph for the March 1968 issue of *Vogue* where she was then editor-in-chief. In it 1960s international star-actress-heiress-beauty Princess Ira von Fürstenberg photographed by Penati wears little more than seven Claflin jeweled dragon brooches dangling from gold chains that encircle her shapely nude torso.

As the 1970s began and the fashion excesses of the 1960s faded into history, Tiffany's hired a young German jewelry designer, Angela Cummings, to work with Claflin.

Cummings, then twenty-six, had first completed her studies in jewelry design at Hanau's prestigious Zeichenakademie (Academy of Design). Her school drawings already showed her deep love affair with the beauty she found in nature's forms and materials and a rare ability to reflect that passion with an innocence, freshness, and simplicity unknown to the 1960s. On the evidence of her student designs alone, Tiffany's chairman Walter Hoving hired her at their first meeting. The timing was perfect. The 1970s longed for a return to basics and had a new-found focus on nature and the environment. This

return to simplicity was, of course, also fueled by a major recession that would see the Dow Jones Industrial Average fall more than 27 percent in 1974, its seventh worst year ever.

Angela Cummings's jewels appeared under her own name as designer in Tiffany's 1975–1976 Blue Book, and fashion gurus like the *New York Post*'s Eugenia Sheppard responded well to Cummings's introduction of nature's intriguing materials like zebrawood, cinnamon wood, and purpleheart mixed with gold and unexpectedly gentle and lyrical combinations of soft-colored semiprecious stones.

"There are lots of things that inspire me," Cummings commented. "Sometimes seasons, sometimes colors. Spring has a certain softness to it, all the colors are very soft."

"There's no nostalgia, either, not even a respectful look back at traditional jewelry, in anything that Angela designs," Eugenia Sheppard added in her "Inside Fashions" column of October 5, 1975. "Her pieces are as contemporary as today's kitchens. Though the exotic materials, the individuality and the fascinating techniques will all appeal to a sophisticated audience."

In the depths of the recession of 1974, Elsa Peretti, the designer who would have the greatest impact on fashion of any jewelry designer of the twentieth century, arrived at Tiffany's. Peretti was no stranger to the New York fashion world. She was the favorite model of Halston, the leading 1970s New York designer, and she was also the darling of such greats of fashion photography as Helmut Newton and Francesco Scavullo. Influential fashion editors such as *Vogue*'s Grace Mirabella and *Harper's Bazaar*'s Carrie Donovan wore her jewelry as did her friend Liza Minnelli, and she had already won fashion's coveted Coty Award.

Her introduction to Tiffany's public in the 1974–1975 Blue Book stated the case for her compelling designs:

> *Sculptured, organic, sensuous, are all words that describe the work of Elsa Peretti, a young jewelry designer with great respect for natural form. What these words do not describe is the simple strength and beauty Miss Peretti achieves with her designs. They are timeless, yet timely; fashionable and at the same time above fashion. They look as handsome when worn as when they are in repose on a flat surface. Finally, they feel as beautiful as they look.* (p. 98)

"She was the one who brought a totally new concept into the jewelry field, making things you want to touch and hold," Diane von Furstenberg, a fellow star of 1970s fashion, observed in the cover story of *Newsweek*'s April 4, 1977, issue titled "Jewelry's New Dazzle."

"Changes in fashion were themselves a major influence on jewelry design." The *Newsweek* article went on to say that "as women retreated to solid-colored sportswear, jewelry became the accessory that made the outfit new and distinctive."

> *These days the crowds head for tiny lopsided golden hearts, gold and silver teardrops, lima-bean-shaped earrings, silver and ivory cuff bracelets and minuscule diamonds dotted along delicate gold chains and sold "by the yard" for necklaces. The landslide success of these unlikely pieces has sparked the most revolutionary changes in serious jewelry since the Renaissance. And oddly enough, it all began at Tiffany's, with the arrival of a tempestuous Italian ex-model named Elsa Peretti.*
>
> *Scion of a wealthy Roman family and a star in the New York fashion galaxy, 36-year-old Elsa Peretti is as elegant and unorthodox as the jewelry she designs. She is equally at home in her chic, all-white mirrored penthouse in New York, on her wooden bench in Tiffany's workshop and at the primitive chicken farm in Spain where she lives four months a year.* (p. 64)

Today, after almost thirty years, Peretti jewelry has achieved a success in the world market undreamt of by any other designer and remains the most frequently illustrated by the fashion press.

The "retreat" to "solid-colored sportswear," however, was over by the 1980s when high-spirited innovators in fashion like Christian Lacroix came into the spotlight.

To answer fashion's rekindled passion for color and opulence Tiffany's introduced the generously scaled and brightly colored jewels of Paloma Picasso in October of 1980.

Paloma Picasso was neither a newcomer to jewelry design nor to the international fashion world. As a teenager in the late 1960s, she collected ethnic jewelry (principally of Hindu and Islamic origin) or glass jewelry from her much-loved and much-frequented Venice. A friend who co-owned the Yves Saint Laurent Rive Gauche store in Venice added Saint Laurent clothes from the stockroom to her wardrobe.

By nineteen she had met Yves Saint Laurent and his business partner Pierre Bergé, and the next year (1970) she began designing her first fashion jewelry for them. Ten years later, after her formal schooling in jewelry design, she was invited to join Tiffany &

HERB RITTS

44

Co. by John Loring, the same friend who fourteen years before had run the Saint Laurent boutique in Venice. He had by then become the design director.

Rigorously avoiding anything in design that hinted of fine-art references, which would inevitably risk unfair comparisons with her father, Paloma Picasso nonetheless encouraged the boldness associated with his Spanish background in her designs that were aggressively chic and strikingly elegant, if often severe.

As the *Washington Post* style reporter, Nina Hyde wrote about her under the heading "Defining a Fashion Boom" in 1988, eight years after her Tiffany & Co. debut when she had become world-famous as a jewelry designer:

> *Picasso believes that one's Hispanic background often comes through in fashion design. With the great Balenciaga, for example, "there was a certain grandeur. A certain elegance. With Spain it is always a mix of something very extreme and also very retenue. . . . Strict and opulent at the same time." For Picasso herself, "there is always an element of classicism in everything that I do, mixed with an element of fun." It shows in the whoppingly popular squiggles and crosses in the jewelry she has designed for Tiffany's. (Washington Post, September 16, 1988)*

With Paloma the marriage of fashion and jewelry design was always exuberant, dramatic, and incontestably elegant, and the Paloma Picasso look gave its own fashion leadership throughout the 1980s and 1990s.

In February of 1991, London's *Sunday Express Magazine*'s Josephine Fairley wrote:

> *Paloma has become renowned globally as a style icon. Paloma it was who recently shook out her collection of psychedelic Pucci blouses, kindling a trend that swept through a million wordrobes like wildfire. It was she who reintroduced the "grown-up handbag," with her accessory collection. Indeed, Paloma's penchant for teaming red with black first inspired countless women to break out of monochrome. But today, as if to underline that she is unerringly at least one season ahead and amid a sea of Palomaesque red jackets, the woman herself is wearing a black and white Chanel suit with shocking pink. (p.27)*

And, even if as Paloma commented further on in the same article, "I resist fashion; I don't like its relentless pace," her jewels are as much in pace with high fashion as the Yves Saint Laurent, Azzedine Alaia, Chanel, Geoffrey Beene, and Bill Blass clothes she herself wears with them.

The pace of fashion, of fashion photography, and of fashion jewels has been relentless since Edward Steichen first put Tiffany jewels in *Vogue* in 1933. All three have evolved with dazzling speed. All joined to produce over the last seven decades a world of stylishness available to a vast audience that once could only have dreamed that the best of fashion and design would be available to them.

The worldwide awareness and enjoyment of fashion that play so great a role in today's lifestyles are forever in debt to the great couturiers, photographers, jewelry designers, magazine editors, fashion writers, and fashion publicists that made it all possible.

Here at Tiffany & Co. we, too, are grateful to all of them and especially to our own designers, Elsa Peretti, Paloma Picasso, and Jean Schlumberger.

SKREBNESKI

STEICHEN

STEICHEN

ANTON BRUEHL

HOYNINGEN-HUENE

STEICHEN

HORST

HOYNINGEN-HUENE

HOYNINGEN-HUENE

STEICHEN

STEICHEN

NELSON

HORST

59

HOYNINGEN-HUENE

HOYNINGEN-HUENE

GEORGE PLATT LYNES

ANTON BRUEHL

HOYNINGEN-HUENE

MAN RAY

MAN RAY

HORST

HORST

69

MEERSON

GEORGE PLATT LYNES

HOYNINGEN-HUENE

STEICHEN

DE MOLAS

LOUISE DAHL-WOLFE

HOYNINGEN-HUENE

STEICHEN

KOLLAR

RUZZIE GREEN

HORST

83

NORDHAUSEN

STEICHEN

HOYNINGEN-HUENE

87

HOYNINGEN-HUENE

LOUISE DAHL-WOLFE

HORST

TONI FRISSELL

HORST

HOYNINGEN-HUENE

HOYNINGEN-HUENE.

HOYNINGEN-HUENE

CECIL BEATON

HORST

ANDRÉ DE DIENES

99

JOFFÉ

100

Christmas 1940

JOHN RAWLINGS

HORST

HORST

DESMOND RUSSELL

KAREN RADKAI

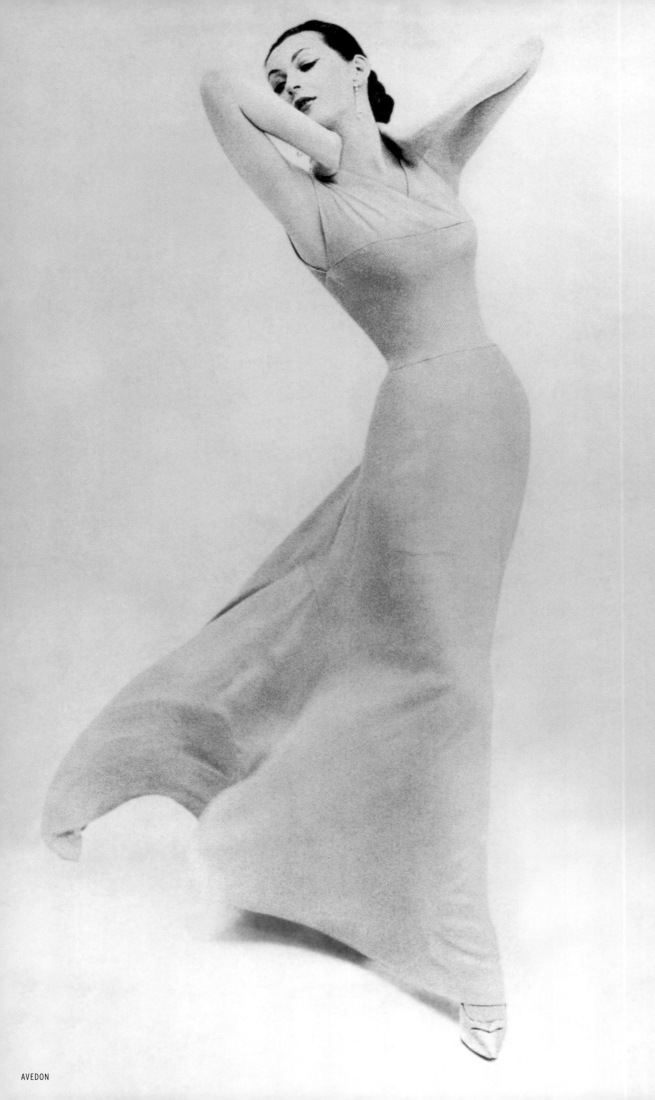

AVEDON

AVEDON

JOHN RAWLINGS

KAREN RADKAI

SAUL LEITER

LOUIS FAURER

AVEDON

PALUMBO

AVEDON

AVEDON

JACQUES LOWE

122

HENRY CLARKE

HIRO

MELVIN SOKOLSKY

BERT STERN

AVEDON

JAMES MOORE

134

JAMES MOORE

SAUL LEITER

HELMUT NEWTON

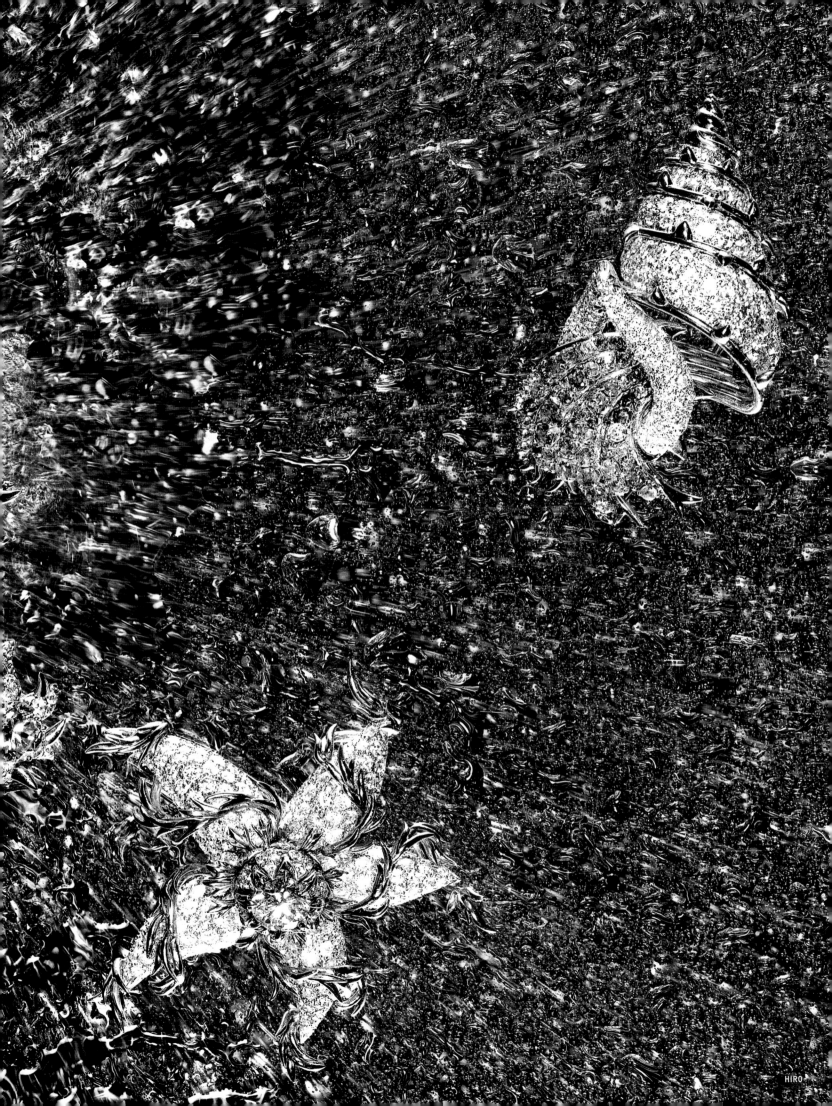

BERT STERN

IRA MAZER

BERT STERN

SILANO

PENATI

SILANO

BERT STERN

HIRO

JAMES MOORE

150

NEAL BARR

HIRO

RYSZARD HOROWITZ

GENE LAURENTS

155

FRANCES MCLAUGHLIN-GILL

156

LOUISVILLE
PACK UP & GO
TO THE
KENTUCKY DERBY

SAUL LEITER

SCAVULLO

BILL KING

159

SCAVULLO

BERT STERN

CHARLES TRACY

165

SCAVULLO

CHRIS VON WANGENHEIM

HILDA MORAY

AVEDON

HIRO

BOB STONE

RICO PUHLMANN

173

JEAN-LOUP SIEFF

STAN MALINOWSKI

BOB RICHARDSON

ALBERTO RIZZO

HIRO

SCAVULLO

SCAVULLO

STAN MALINOWSKI

STAN MALINOWSKI

185

SKREBNESKI

189

HIRO

ERIC BOMAN

SKREBNESKI

SKREBNESKI

195

SKREBNESKI

SKREBNESKI

198

BILL KING

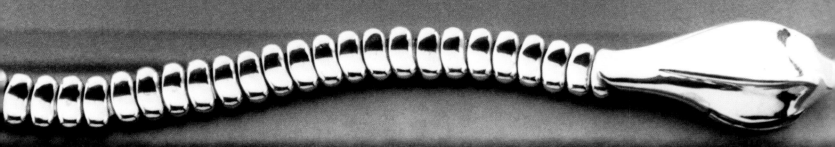

SKREBNESKI

SCAVULLO

KENRO IZU

MARC HISPARD

SHEILA METZNER

SCAVULLO

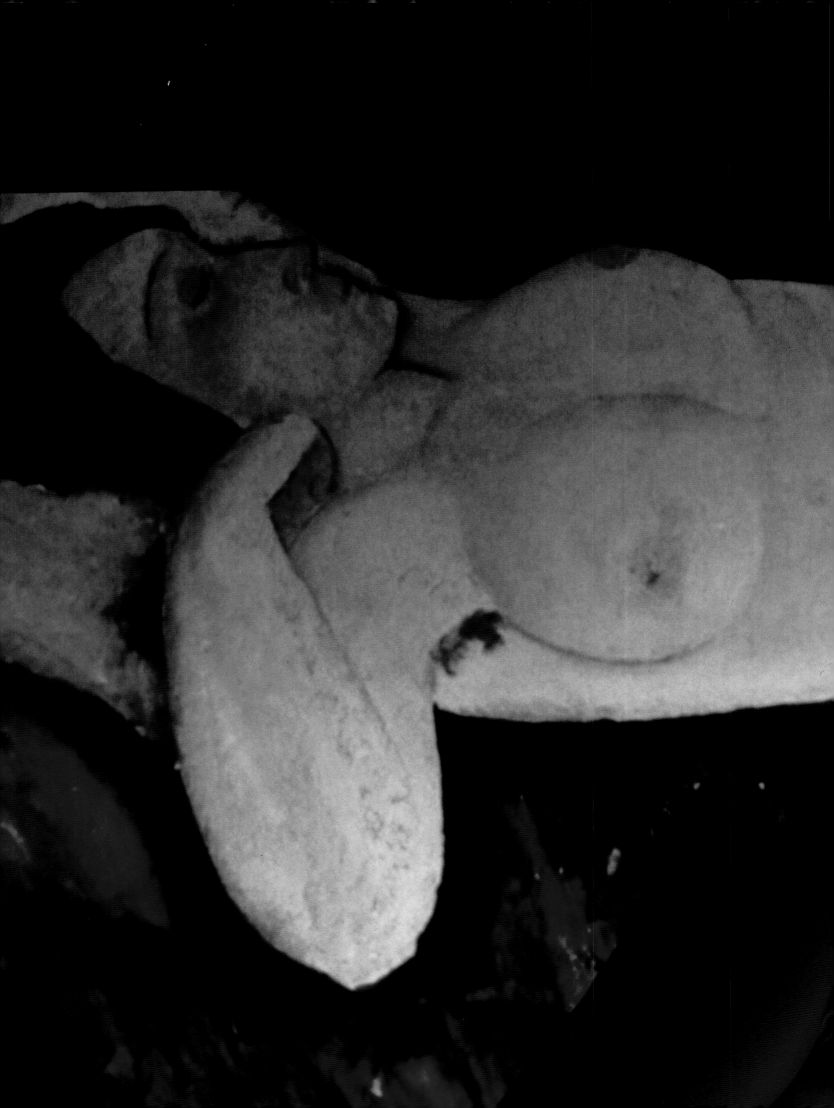

SKREBNESKI

SKREBNESKI

SHEILA METZNER

ALBERT WATSON

ALBERT WATSON

SKREBNESKI

BILL KING

PETER BEARD

RICO PUHLMANN

FABRIZIO FERRI

DAVID LACHAPELLE

SCAVULLO

SCAVULLO

GILLES BENSIMON

ALBERT WATSON

GREG KADEL

CHRIS CRAYMER

KARINA TAÏRA

JEFF RIEDEL

PATRICK DEMARCHELIER

List of Illustrations

Numbers preceding the entries
refer to page numbers.

Endpaper, left: Edward Steichen's photograph of Gwili André wearing a gold lamé evening dress by Omar Kiam and Tiffany jewels in *Vogue*'s October 15, 1940, issue. The "Comet" brooch of rubies and diamonds and the morganite and diamond bracelet (priced at $65,000) were included in Tiffany's exhibit at the 1939–40 World's Fair held in Flushing Meadows, New York. The Luxembourg-born, American-raised Edward Steichen (1879–1973) spent his formative years in Paris; he returned to New York in 1923 and became the chief photographer for *Vanity Fair* and for *Vogue*, a position he retained until 1938. He later became the Museum of Modern Art's photography curator.

Endpaper, right: Another Steichen photograph from *Vogue*'s October 15, 1940, issue shows Gwili André in a V-necked black crêpe satin dress from Bergdorf Goodman; the hat, coiffure, and dress were influenced by Olivia de Havilland's costumes in the role of Melanie in *Gone with the Wind*, released in 1939. André also wears a Tiffany diamond bracelet and four emerald-and-diamond clips that were part of a tiara that Tiffany's made for the 1939–40 New York World's Fair to display a 75-carat emerald (see page 104).

1: *Vogue*'s November 1, 1944, cover shows aquamarine-and-diamond earrings from Tiffany's and a man's profile in silhouette. The caption reads, "Across the face of beauty is the shadow of a man . . . even a man across the sea. His influence keeps her heart warm . . . her eyes bright. Against The Day of his return, she is her beauty's guardian." The photograph-montage was by Erwin Blumenfeld (1897–1968), who was born in Berlin and began taking fashion photographs in Paris in 1937. He was interned as an enemy alien when Germany invaded France; after his release he managed to emigrate, and Carmel Snow of *Harper's Bazaar* hired him the day after he arrived in New York in August 1941.

2–3: *Harper's Bazaar*'s December 1939 issue captioned this Hoyningen-Huene (studio-shot) beach scene, "For nights under the Southern Cross." The "rose-orchid" organza and satin sheath was by Germaine Monteil, a fashionable New York designer of the 1930s later known for her cosmetics and perfumes. The jewels are from Tiffany's. Baron George Hoyningen-Huene (1900–1968) was born in Saint Petersburg; after the Russian Revolution he became a successful commercial artist and photographer for *Vanity Fair* and *Vogue* in Paris, where he also designed the lighting for African American singer Bricktop's Paris nightclub. He left *Vogue* for *Harper's Bazaar* in 1935 at the behest of Alexey Brodovitch (1898–1971), another Russian émigré, who had joined *Harper's Bazaar* in 1934; Brodovitch remained at the magazine until 1958 and was called "the art director of the century." In the 1950s and 1960s Hoyningen-Huene was a color coordinator in Hollywood, where his credits include *A Star is Born* starring Judy Garland (1954). He also designed the costumes for *A Breath of Scandal* starring Sophia Loren (1960).

4–5: Horst's photograph in *Vogue*'s October 15, 1936, issue shows a beveled-rectangle aquamarine ring and aquamarine-and-diamond bracelets from Tiffany's. The caption reads, "Aquamarines—limpid, glacial as the waters of a Northern lake—to play against a dress of white satin or the palest mauve mousseline." The German-born Horst P. Horst (1906–1999) began his long career in photography as the protégé of Hoyningen-Huene, whom he met in Paris in 1930. Barbara Martin recently wrote, "Huene and Horst contributed to the invention of the fashion photograph as a dynamic artistic statement rather than simply an image of costly clothing. Elegant and idealized, their photographs are studio creations wrought with an understanding of the careful adjustment of pose and lighting requiring two or three seconds and calculated without a light meter. As Horst said later, 'Women didn't flaunt their emotions when photographed by Steichen or Man Ray or Huene. . . . They were pensive, self-absorbed, seemingly oblivious of the world around them. The change came with the advent of fast film, after World War Two.'" Barbara Martin, "The Look: Images of Glamour and Style," Museum of Fine Arts, Boston, 2001).

6: In its July 1, 1933, issue *Vogue* ran its first photograph featuring Tiffany jewelry, showing Broadway actress Katherine Leslie (Mrs. Julien Chaqueneau in private life) at a mirrored dressing table—set with silver from Tiffany's—wearing a tea gown

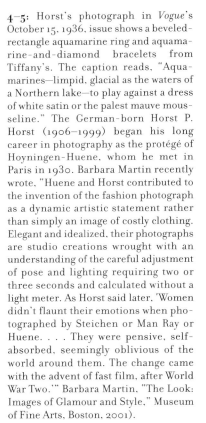

from Bergdorf Goodman. Fashionable women of the time wore tea gowns when receiving guests at home. Photograph by Steichen.

9: *Harper's Bazaar* captioned this Hoyningen-Huene photograph in its May 1936 issue, "The tea-gown descending the staircase was designed by Mainbocher to be one of the greatest pleasures of an evening at home. It is green taffeta shot with violet, and it has a skirt that is short and full at the front and carried on into a train at back. The sleeves are deeply puffed, like the ones you see in 1893 albums of the Crown Heads of Europe, and the only ornament is a bunch of violets." The diamond necklace—centered by a cabochon sapphire—and the diamond bracelet are from Tiffany's.

10: Hattie Carnegie "sailor hats" and dresses with Tiffany clips on the necklines. (The clips at right also appear on page 13.) Photographed by Steichen for *Vogue*'s May 1, 1936, issue. Hattie Carnegie (1887–1956) was born Henrietta Kanengeiser in Vienna. She and her family moved to New York City's Lower East Side in 1892, and she started work as a messenger for Macy's in 1904. Five years later she Americanized her image by using a professional name resonating with ideas of wealth, success, and philanthropy, and she opened a hatshop on Manhattan's East Tenth Street. By 1923 she was on Forty-ninth Street off Park Avenue, where she reigned over American fashion into the 1950s: her specialties were "little Carnegie suits" and elegant evening dresses.

13: Hat by Lilly Daché photographed by Steichen for *Vogue*'s May 1, 1936, issue. The sheer crêpe checked suit was from Estelle-Mildred (MGM's Gilbert Adrian had introduced checked gingham suits about 1934). The model wears a Tiffany diamond clip at the neck, a diamond-and-black-enamel bracelet (priced at $2,250), and a diamond and quartz ring ($300). Quartz became fashionable in fine jewelry in the mid-1930s and paved the way for the mixture of precious and nonprecious materials in "fashion jewelry." Lilly Daché worked for a milliner in Paris before coming to New York in 1924; she opened her first hat shop in 1926. Twelve years later she constructed her own seven-story building at 14 East Fifty-sixth Street, where she had 150 employees.

14: Dianne de Witt modeling Paloma Picasso's gold necklace with a 251-carat citrine pendant, photographed by Michael Halsband for *Ultra*'s October 1987 issue.

15: Hoyningen-Huene's photograph for *Harper's Bazaar*'s October 1940 issue shows a watch of diamonds and rubies set in gold with matching ear clips. The architectural model was made from Leonardo da Vinci's 1483 drawing for an ideal city; it was on exhibit at the 1939–40 New York World's Fair.

17: Richard Avedon's photograph in *Harper's Bazaar*'s October 1957 issue shows a James Galanos dress and Tiffany earrings. It is captioned, "Here is how you can look humanly warm and cool and ladylike all at the same time. After you've picked an effective dress and realized that you're about to face the challenging, underwater-cavern effects of nightclub lighting." After serving in the American merchant marine during World War II, Avedon studied at the New School under Alexey Brodovitch, who hired him as a staff photographer for *Harper's Bazaar* in 1946. Avedon soon became the most successful fashion photographer in history. His career inspired Fred Astaire's role in the 1957 movie musical *Funny Face*; Kay Thompson's supporting role was based on Diana Vreeland, and Avedon himself was a special visual consultant for the film. Galanos was trained in New York, became a sketch artist for Columbia Pictures costume designer Jean Louis, then worked in Paris and New York. He opened his first shop in Beverly Hills in 1951 and won the Coty Award in 1954. Until his retirement in 2000 he was California's leading fashion designer, celebrated for superbly elegant haute couture designs.

19: Prominent New York socialite Countess Consuelo Crespi photographed by Gleb Derujinsky for *Town & Country*'s June 1956 issue in the Palm Court of the Plaza Hotel wearing a Tiffany diamond brooch and a short evening dress by James Galanos; the caption described its linen bodice as "carved low in back, rising more demurely to a low bateau neck. The skirt is a minutely-gathered sweep of satin-striped Stoffel voile." Consuelo Crespi's husband, Rudi, was instrumental in bringing Italian fashion to New York.

20: Madeleine Vionnet's superbly elegant black satin slip evening dress with a soft cowl neckline and net overskirt embroidered in paillettes, worn here with a Tiffany aquamarine ring, a diamond clip, and four bracelets; the jewels' total value was $57,975. Photographed by Martin Munkacsi for *Harper's Bazaar*'s November 1937 issue. *Harper's* commented, "Black is never all black this winter . . . by night it is set on fire by a touch of gold or the sparkle of paillettes or by masses of multicolored jewels." Vionnet (1876–1975)

was the greatest couturière of the 1930s: her revolutionary bias cut gave new fluidity to the hang of fabric, and the closing of her salon after the Germans occupied Paris in 1940 was a serious loss to fashion. Christian Dior, her leading post–World War II successor, remarked, "No one has ever carried the art of dressmaking further than Vionnet." The Hungarian-born photographer Munkacsi (1896–1963) was a news and sports photographer in Budapest and Berlin before Hearst Publications hired him in 1934. He is credited with originating the energetic, outdoor look in fashion photography, as well as the use of extreme angles, shooting upward from ground level or downward from a ladder.

24–25: Paramount Pictures' stars photographed by Eugene Robert Richee wearing simulated pearl necklaces imitating the fabulously expensive "Ropes of Pearls" advertised by Tiffany & Co. in the 1920s. Page 24, top: Esther Ralston (1928). Page 24, bottom: Olga Baclanova (1927) in a costume by Howard Greer, one of Hollywood's all-time great designers. Page 25: Louise Brooks (1928).

26: Princess Xenia of Russia wearing a black-and-white zigzag crêpe dress by Jessie Franklin Turner and a fortune in Tiffany diamond bracelets. The first society fashion portrait with Tiffany jewelry was photographed for *Harper's Bazaar*'s June 1933 issue by Toni von Horn. In 1923 Wall Street banker Otto Kahn brought Baroness Antonie "Toni" von Horn (1899–1970) from Germany—both were from Mannheim—to photograph "Oneka," his estate on Long Island. Not long afterward *Vanity Fair* editor Frank Crowninshield encouraged her to take up fashion photography; her studio was above the 21 Club (then a speakeasy) at 21 West Fifty-second Street. Princess Xenia (1903–1965) was a great-granddaughter of Czar Nicholas I and a niece of King Constantine I of Greece; three years before von Horn took this photograph, Princess Xenia had divorced William Bateman Leeds, Jr., heir to a large tin-plating fortune. Jessie Franklin Turner worked in the custom salon at Bonwit Teller before opening her own shop in 1922 on West Fifty-seventh Street, specializing in tea gowns made of exotic fabrics.

28: The January 1934 issue of *Harper's Bazaar* included a portfolio photographed by Toni von Horn titled "Four Evenings in the Life of Mrs. Allan Ryan, Junior." Here Janet Ryan wears a magnificent sable cape from Jaeckel, an evening dress in two tones of gray crêpe from Saks Fifth Avenue's Salon Mod-

erne, a Tiffany diamond bandeau (also shown on page 29, and Tiffany diamond bracelets. Allan Ryan was a grandson of New York financier Thomas Fortune Ryan.

29: Tiffany jewelry photographed for *Vogue*'s December 1, 1933 (Christmas), issue by Anton Bruehl. These Art Deco–style jewels, probably designed at Tiffany's Paris branch, are strikingly different from those made under the direction of Louis Comfort Tiffany, who had died eleven months before. Preferring semiprecious stones, Louis Comfort Tiffany seldom featured diamonds, rubies, or emeralds in his jewelry; yet all these pieces are entirely composed of these precious stones. The most important jewels are the diamond necklace with carved emeralds at left, the diamond bracelet with five rubies at center, the diamond bandeau (hair ornament) at upper right, the bracelet with a stripe of square emeralds mounted with nine large emerald-cut diamonds, and the hat pin with diamonds surrounding a carved emerald at bottom right. Bruehl (1900–1982) was born in Australia and opened his New York photograph studio in 1925. He was a pioneer in color photography: he and Fernand Bourges reformulated Condé Nast Publications' color engraving process in the early 1930s, when magazine color photographs were rare. Bruehl took many fashion photographs for *Vogue* and was later well-known for industrial photography.

31: An early color photograph by Steichen for *Vogue*'s November 1, 1933, issue featuring a wide-brimmed dinner hat and gloves by John-Frederics, a dress by Gervais, and a ring, diamond clip, and important diamond bracelets from Tiffany's. *Vogue* commented, "Let your hat be as large as you like for dinner—let it be some sort of eye-shadowing, allure-spelling picture such as this one of black velvet, with a streak of green velvet across the crown."

32: This photograph by Toni von Horn for *Harper's Bazaar* January 1934 issue shows Janet Ryan wearing three Tiffany bracelets and Jeanne Lanvin's gold lamé top and slim black skirt with gold lamé straps; the ensemble included a matching gold lamé jacket. Lanvin (1867–1946) played a leading role in haute couture from the time she opened her first Paris shop in 1889. In 1915 *Vogue* commented, "She has never departed from her first conviction that modified Grecian lines are the best for the youthful figure." At the 1925 Exposition des Art Décoratifs et Industriels Moderne, Lanvin's partner, decorator Armand Albert Rateau, designed a bedroom for her that elevated the Art Deco style to the height of fashion. In 1925 and 1927 Lanvin created "My Sin" and "Arpège," hugely successful perfumes with Rateau-designed bottles. In the 1930s her clients included Hollywood stars Mary Pickford and Marlene Dietrich. Her daughter, Countess Jean de Polignac, carried on Lanvin's couture and perfume businesses after World War II.

33: Janet Ryan wearing Tiffany bracelets and a white chiffon gown with printed pastel bouquets designed by Bernard Newman of Bergdorf Goodman; *Harper's Bazaar* called it "as fresh and naive as the wall-paper in a country house." The photograph is by Toni von Horn.

34   35

34: *Harper's Bazaar*'s November 1935 issue featured important Tiffany & Co. jewelry. On her left hand the model wears a cabochon sapphire ring priced at $21,200, on her left wrist, a diamond bracelet priced at $55,500. In the photograph that she is holding, she has the platinum blonde, swept-back coffure popularized by film goddess Carole Lombard, and she wears an unusual diamond earring "which encircles her ear." This dressing-table scene was shot by Hoyningen-Huene.

35: Two magnificent "American Deco" necklaces that Tiffany & Co. made for the New York World's Fair 1939–40, photographed by Anton Bruehl for *Vogue*'s June 15, 1939, issue. The sapphire, diamond, and gold necklace at the top had detachable side elements that could be worn as clips (it was priced at a modest $1,400). The diamond and platinum necklace at bottom featured a 217.57-carat aquamarine from Brazil's Santa Maria Mine (it was priced at $28,000).

36   37

36–37: *Town & Country*'s December 1935 issue included this photo by Emelie Danielson showing Tiffany jewelry. The necklace and bracelet on the wrist at bottom left are set with pillow-shaped cabochon Maine tourmalines accented with small diamonds. They were designed by Meta Overbeck under Louis Comfort Tiffany's direction circa 1930. The only photograph of Louis Comfort Tiffany's jewelry to appear in a fashion magazine, it was published nearly three years after his death. The bracelet is now in Tiffany & Co.'s Permanent Collection.

38   39

38: Man Ray (1890–1976) was born in Philadelphia and had his first one-man painting show in New York in 1912. He and Marcel Duchamp founded the New York Dada movement in 1917; in 1921 he moved to Paris, where he became a leader of the Surrealist movement and began photographing Paul Poiret's fash-

ions for *Vogue*. He moved to *Harper's Bazaar* at Alexey Brodovitch's urging in 1934. In the 1920s Man Ray had invented Rayographs, abstract images made by placing objects on photosensitive surfaces; his photograph of Tiffany jewels for *Harper's Bazaar*'s 1936 December issue is in the style of a Rayograph. Center: A necklace of round rose-cut diamonds priced at $30,300. Upper left: A black pearl and diamond ring priced at $14,400. Center, top and bottom: A pair of diamond clips priced at $4,500. Upper right: A yellow diamond sunburst brooch priced at $815. Bottom, left and right: A pair of diamond hoop earrings priced at $510.

39: Patricia Neal was famous in the early 1950s for her role in *The Fountainhead* (1949) opposite Gary Cooper. In this photograph she posed for Ivan Dmitri at Tiffany & Co.'s New York store for a January 31, 1953, *Saturday Evening Post* story about the company. The emerald brooch on page 104 is on the table at lower left. Patricia Neal was later acclaimed for her supporting role in *Breakfast at Tiffany's* (1961) and her Academy Award–winning performance in *Hud* (1963).

40: *Town & Country*'s February 1957 issue featured Dina Merrill, photographed by Stephen Colhoun, calling her "A young television actress who has a definite taste for simple and casual clothes that don't dominate. Here she wears a costume she loves: Ben Zuckerman's easy suit of Coudurier mauve tweed, with matching silk-surah blouse. The jacket has four patch pockets; the skirt is slim. The carnation clip and gold link bracelets are from Tiffany." Dina Merrill subsequently appeared in many films; she is the daughter of Marjorie Merriwether Post, the most extravagant American society woman of all time. Ben Zuckerman was born in Romania, came to New York as a child, and began working in the garment industry in his teens. He opened his own business in 1951 and won three Coty Awards in the 1950s.

40   41

41: High-society beauty CZ Guest (wife of Winston Guest, one of America's leading polo players), wearing a Tiffany necklace by Jean Schlumberger with a gray flannel dress and a ranch-mink waist-length "barrel" jacket, both by Mainbocher, in the December 1956 issue of *Town & Country*. (Jean Schlumberger and Tiffany's had joined forces nine months earlier.) Photographed here by Stephen Colhoun, CZ Guest, celebrated as one of the best dressed of America's social figures, later wrote columns for *Vogue* and gardening advice for the *New York Post*. Mainbocher (1891–1976) was born in Chicago and moved to Europe in 1911. In 1930 he opened a haute couture salon in Paris; his most prominent client was Wallis Warfield Simpson, for whom he designed the "Wallis blue" dress that she wore at her wedding to the Duke of Windsor (formerly King Edward VIII) in 1937. Mainbocher moved to New York in 1939, and his designs remained in fashion until he retired in 1971.

43: Elsa Peretti, modeling an outfit by Halston and her "Equestrian" silver belt buckle at a 1973 showing for fashion writers: Bernadine Morris of the *New York Times* is second from left. Peretti based this buckle on her oversize faux ivory buckle shown on page 163; it was derived from a buckle on a harness she saw in Mexico.

44: Paloma Picasso wearing her necklace of natural baroque South Sea pearls with a pendant set with a 396-carat kunzite in a diamond-pavé gold ribbon, photographed by Herb Ritts for Italian *Vogue*'s December 1996 issue. The necklace is now on display in the Janet Annenberg Hooker Hall of Geology, Gems, and Minerals at the Smithsonian Institution's Museum of Natural History.

46–47: Victor Skrebneski's photograph of a silk charmeuse robe by Josie Natori with Paloma Picasso's gold-link collar centered by a 50-carat amethyst and gold chain with a 42-carat citrine pendant. From *Town & Country*'s February 1992 issue.

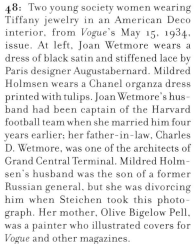

48: Two young society women wearing Tiffany jewelry in an American Deco interior, from *Vogue*'s May 15, 1934, issue. At left, Joan Wetmore wears a dress of black satin and stiffened lace by Paris designer Augustabernard. Mildred Holmsen wears a Chanel organza dress printed with tulips. Joan Wetmore's husband had been captain of the Harvard football team when she married him four years earlier; her father-in-law, Charles D. Wetmore, was one of the architects of Grand Central Terminal. Mildred Holmsen's husband was the son of a former Russian general, but she was divorcing him when Steichen took this photograph. Her mother, Olive Bigelow Pell, was a painter who illustrated covers for *Vogue* and other magazines.

49: Steichen's photograph on the facing page of *Vogue*'s May 15, 1934, issue shows Jane Swope wearing Tiffany jewelry and a white chiffon gown with huge blue polka dots from Worth in Paris. Jane Swope was the daughter of Herbert Bayard Swope, a Pulitzer Prize–winning newspaper reporter and editor, who backed Franklin Delano Roosevelt's

candidacy for president in 1932; in 1934 he became chairman of the New York State Racing Commission. Three months after Steichen took this photograph, Jane Swope married Robert Lee Brandt, a member of the staff of FDR's National Recovery Administration.

50: Madeleine Vionnet's plum satin gown and ermine cape heightened by Tiffany diamond bracelets, choker, clips, and solitaire ring, photographed by Anton Bruehl for *Vogue*'s October 15, 1935, issue. *Vogue*'s caption noted, "Blue-white diamonds demand a regal background." The décor was by the celebrated interior designer Elsie de Wolfe (Lady Charles Mendl).

51: The model reclines seductively in a Hollywood glamour portrait pose on a polar bear rug wearing Bergdorf Goodman's black velvet jacket, silver lamé trousers gathered at the ankles (later called harem pants), two diamond bracelets and a diamond ring from Tiffany's. Photographed by Hoyningen-Huene for *Harper's Bazaar*'s December 1935 issue.

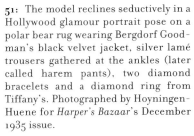

52: Steichen's moving study of femininity in black and gray with Tiffany jewels and minaudière for *Vogue*'s April 15, 1936, issue. Left: an evening dress by Paris couturiere Louiseboulanger; *Vogue* commented, "Layers and layers of tulle belling out over a slim slip, long sleeves, and ruffled shoulders give the black dress its verve." Right: Mainbocher's "rather Anna Kareninish" light gray crêpe dress with a cascade of ruffles. Gilbert Adrian designed the costumes for the 1935 MGM version of Tolstoy's *Anna Karenina* starring Greta Garbo and had a significant influence on fashion in New York and Paris.

53: Paris couturiere Maggy Rouff's sheath of pale cyclamen crêpe and Tiffany jewels, photographed by Horst for *Vogue*'s January 1, 1936, issue. Maggy Rouff (c. 1900–1971) opened her haute couture house in the Champs Elysées in 1930; she also lectured on fashion in the United States and wrote *The Philosophy of Elegance*. In private life she was the socially prominent Mme. Pierre Besançon de Wagner. Here Horst used an exceptionally stylish gold- and silver-leaf Venetian Rococo revival shell chair to set off the shirring of Rouff's sheath.

54: Hoyningen-Huene's photograph in the July 1936 issue of *Harper's Bazaar* shows twenty-year-old blonde heiress Ethel du Pont wearing a white "calla lily" satin dress from Stein and Blaine with ear clips and a $1000 diamond bracelet from Tiffany's shown at above right. White was a fashion obsession in the

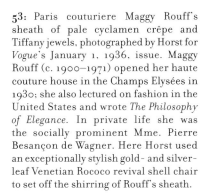

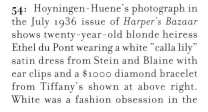

1930s: Hollywood's Adrian declared, "White brings men to women's feet" (*Vogue*, July 1, 1937, p. 22). Ethel du Pont's much-publicized wedding to Franklin Delano Roosevelt, Jr. (the president's eldest son), took place on June 30, 1937; one newspaper reporter described her as "a princess in gossamer white."

55: Hoyningen-Huene's photograph on the facing page of *Harper's Bazaar*'s July 1936 issue shows British film actress Elizabeth Jenns wearing a white sheath; *Harper's* commented that it was "[m]ade for the tall—a very tailored sheer crepe, buttoned with four gold buttons and belted with gold kid—the taller you are the better for these long plain graceful lines." Jenns also wears Tiffany diamond bracelets and a pair of Tiffany diamond clips priced at $500 each. One clip is shown at above left; *Harper's* called it "a fabulous waterfall of diamonds flexibly set in pieces like great pure cold drops of water."

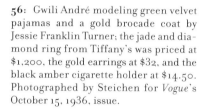

56   57

56: Gwili André modeling green velvet pajamas and a gold brocade coat by Jessie Franklin Turner; the jade and diamond ring from Tiffany's was priced at $1,200, the gold earrings at $32, and the black amber cigarette holder at $14.50. Photographed by Steichen for *Vogue*'s October 15, 1936, issue.

57: In this Steichen photograph for *Vogue*'s August 1, 1936, issue, André wears a blue wool suit and a black felt toque by Descat with "propeller" quills (inspired by Suzy, the leading milliner in Paris) as well as a large Tiffany star sapphire ring and dramatic gold bracelets. Star sapphires frequently appeared on solitaire rings during the Great Depression, when fewer Tiffany clients could afford large, faceted precious stones.

58   59

58: This photograph by Lusha Nelson in *Vogue*'s July 15, 1936, issue shows a model at an American Deco dressing table applying perfume from Tiffany's sterling silver vanity case while wearing a Chanel black net evening dress and Tiffany bracelets. (This vanity case is now on display at Boston's Museum of Fine Arts.) Hollywood's still photographers often shot movie stars at their dressing tables.

59: Horst's photograph for *Vogue*'s October 15, 1936, issue features a diamond-and-emerald ring, a diamond bracelet, and a jeweled compact from Tiffany's. *Vogue* commented, "Big stones are enormously smart—if they're as superbly cut and mounted as the diamonds on the bracelet."

60: Madeleine Vionnet's wide silver lamé evening dress with a black Chantilly lace "Mary Stuart mantle," photographed by Hoyningen-Huene for *Harper's Bazaar*'s October 1936 issue. (The film of Maxwell Anderson's *Mary of Scotland* starring Katharine Hepburn was released in 1936.) The ring—featuring an unusually large natural pearl—is from Tiffany's branch in Paris.

60   61

61: Vionnet's halter neck evening dress with an enormous black silk net skirt with net rosettes, photographed by Hoyningen-Huene for *Harper's Bazaar*'s October 1936 issue. The model wears an important Tiffany diamond bracelet on her right arm.

62: Black velvet evening dress from Bonwit Teller, a gold snake belt, zebra-stripe sandals, and a Tiffany diamond bracelet priced at $30,200, photographed by George Platt Lynes for *Harper's Bazaar*'s November 1936 issue. George Platt Lynes (1907–1955) first exhibited his still-life photographs in the "Surréalism" show at Julien Levy's New York gallery in 1934.

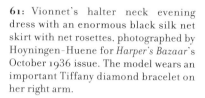

62   63

63: George Platt Lynes's photograph of London and Paris designer Edward Molyneux's black shirred Valenciennes lace evening dress with a hoop skirt appeared in *Harper's Bazaar*'s April 1937 issue. The bracelets are from Tiffany's branch in Paris. Lynes's work was often highly mannered: here his model has an dancer's pose and painted clouds at her feet. In the late 1930s Lynes was the official photographer of the American Ballet Company.

64: Anton Bruehl's photograph in *Vogue*'s December 15, 1936, issue shows a Lanvin dress, a sable cape, and a Tiffany diamond necklace priced at $26,400. *Vogue* described the Tiffany clip on the neckline as "a festoon of marquise and square diamonds with pear-shaped diamonds falling like drops of liquid fire in a cluster in front. With this a new scroll clip of diamonds that deftly holds the drapery of Lanvin's silk crêpe dress." The clip was priced at $19,975.

64   65

65: Madeleine Vionnet's crinoline of black net with bands of chenille photographed by Hoyningen-Huene for *Harper's Bazaar*'s May 1936 issue. The diamond bracelets are Tiffany's.

66: Man Ray's photograph of the twenty-three-year-old Mary Rogers (actress and daughter of humorist and American institution Will Rogers) wearing Tiffany jewelry and a two-piece white lamé evening dress with rhinestone buttons, from *Harper's Bazaar*'s December 1936 issue. *Harper's* called the dress's

66   67

70   71

color "iridium-white": iridium is a metallic element alloyed with platinum to make jewelry, and in the late 1930s "platinum blondes" and iridium were at the height of popularity—New York's St. Regis Hotel opened a nightclub called the Iridium Room with an ice-skating show starring Dorothy Lewis. White evening dresses were part of this craze: in its July 1, 1937, issue *Vogue* declared, "No color can compete with white in the Paris mid-season," and in its June 15, 1939, issue *Vogue* reported, "White appears again to be Glamour Colour No. 1 for evening. At the opening of the St. Regis Roof, both Mrs. John J. Astor and Mrs. Bryon Foy in white chiffon, three women in Chanel's white lace; one woman in white muslin with black velvet waist streamers."

67: Another Man Ray photograph of Mary Rogers on the facing page of *Harper's Bazaar*'s December 1936 issue. Here she wears Tiffany bracelet and an evening dress with white silk net and mousseline roses; the dress was designed by Sally Milgrim after Madeleine Vionnet (see Vionnet's similar dress on page 61). Milgrim began her career with a custom shop on Manhattan's Lower East Side in the early 1920s; in 1927 she moved to West Fifty-seventh Street. Her best-known work was the light blue gown Eleanor Roosevelt wore to her husband's first inaugural ball in 1933. Milgrim also designed for actresses such as Pearl White, Mary Pickford, Ethel Merman, and Marilyn Miller. At one point she and her husband owned nine specialty shops around the country. She died in 1994 at the age of 103.

68: Helen Forbes made her singing debut at the St. Regis Hotel in 1936. In this Horst photograph from *Vogue*'s July 1, 1937, issue, she wears a sheer black chiffon dress, a shiny black straw hat by Sally Milgrim, and Tiffany's ruby-and-diamond clip and 14-karat gold cuff bracelet with detachable clips set with a large cabochon emerald, three cabochon sapphires, and twenty diamonds. (The bracelet is now in Tiffany & Co.'s Permanent Collection.) Helen Forbes's father was Warren Delano Robbins, a career diplomat whom his cousin Franklin Delano Roosevelt appointed minister to Canada. Her husband was Alexander C. Forbes, a scion of one of Boston's richest families.

69: Horst's photograph from *Vogue*'s July 1, 1937, issue shows Dorothy Paley wearing a black chiffon dress with a pleated white front and massed Tiffany bracelets from which hang her collection of antique seals. Dorothy Paley was then a successful interior decorator, and she

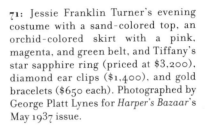

72   73

was on the best-dressed list in 1940; her husband, William S. Paley, had bought CBS in 1928 and turned it into a broadcasting giant. Her first husband was John Randolph Hearst (a son of publishing magnate William Randolph Hearst), and she subsequently married stockbroker Walter Hirshon. Dorothy Hirshon was a leading figure in New York's charitable and social service organizations until the mid-1990s.

70: Black satin evening dress with a jagged hem and train from Saks Fifth Avenue (probably designed by Sophie of Saks [Sophie Gimbel]), photographed by Harry Ossip Meerson for *Harper's Bazaar*'s August 1937 issue. Tiffany's priced the four diamond bracelets on the model's left wrist at a total of $24,550. (In *Harper's* November 1937 issue's "Why don't you—" column, Diana Vreeland wrote, "Appear with all the jewels on the left side, diamonds set in platinum.") Meerson (1910–1991) was born in Russia, moved to Paris in 1929, and began fashion photography in 1932. In later years he was a successful portrait photographer.

71: Jessie Franklin Turner's evening costume with a sand-colored top, an orchid-colored skirt with a pink, magenta, and green belt, and Tiffany's star sapphire ring (priced at $3,200), diamond ear clips ($1,400), and gold bracelets ($650 each). Photographed by George Platt Lynes for *Harper's Bazaar*'s May 1937 issue.

72: Hoyningen-Huene's photograph for *Harper's Bazaar*'s November 1940 issue showing a "biblical-look" wool jersey dress by Nettie Rosenstein accented with Tiffany diamond necklaces and bracelets; the two bracelets were priced at a total of $60,500. Madeleine Vionnet introduced "biblical look" evening dresses with head draperies of satin and silk crêpe in her February 1937 collection. Nettie Rosenstein had a long career in American fashion; she opened her first dressmaking shop in 1918, retired in 1927, then reestablished her company in 1930. Until 1934 her dresses were sold under the names of the stores that carried them; one writer explained that retailers "usually endeavored to give their salons the Paris feeling. . . . It would scarcely enhance that feeling if they were to announce that many of their most irresistible dresses were designed by Nettie Rosenstein in West Forty-seventh Street in New York. . . ."

73: The gold tint of Steichen's photograph for *Vogue*'s October 15, 1937, issue followed the theme set by editor Edna Woolman Chase's "Greed for Gold" feature. Steichen's favorite model, Gwili

André, wears a Tiffany sapphire clip on the turban by John-Frederics, and multiple diamond and emerald bracelets and diamond rings from Tiffany's. The glamorous and modernist 1937 Paris Exposition des Arts et Techniques included large-scale gold jewels and gold-leafed wrought-iron and steel furniture. Chase decreed, "Nothing strikes such a false note in this day and age as dinky, small-fry jewels. . . . The real thing . . . is enormous, entertaining, ornamental, personal, and witty. . . . Again there's a great greed for gold—rich yellow gold and hoards of it. No little gram-weight nuggets content this age—your jewel pieces will be huge and affluent. . . . There's a free attitude about jewels today—just as about clothes—the only law is to be profligate. . . ."

74: The model wears a green velvet evening dress trimmed with kolinsky (an Asian mink) and an overscaled gem-accented floral gold necklace, photographed by George Platt Lynes for *Harper's Bazaar*'s November 1938 issue. Following the example of large-scale floral jewelry at the 1937 Paris Exposition des Arts et Techniques, Tiffany designer Augustus C. Haus began to develop American Deco jewelry under Arthur Leroy Barney's supervision for the 1939–40 New York World's Fair. The background is a fifteenth-century Flemish tapestry from William Randolph Hearst's collection on display at the Parish-Watson Gallery on East Fifty-seventh Street in New York. Hearst, whose forty-five publications included *Harper's Bazaar*, was undergoing financial difficulties because of the Great Depression.

75: Left: a Sally Milgrim dress of faille taffeta with a bodice covered with jet and the back cut like a brassiere. Right: striped mauve taffeta dress trimmed with black velvet from Stein and Blaine. Also photographed by George Platt Lynes for *Harper's Bazaar*'s November 1938 issue in front of another fifteenth-century Flemish tapestry from Hearst's collection.

76: This De Molas photograph in *Vogue*'s May 1, 1939, World's Fair issue is captioned, "5 P.M. TO 2 A.M.—AT THE FAIR. If your evening begins early, with dinner and dancing, and ends late (the amusement curfew rings at two) wear sheer black or brown. Or, if you'd rather stay in town, Mary Martin is singing at the Rainbow Room." Left: black straw hat, soft black chiffon dress with inserts of black lace, and a pearl necklace and clip. Right: pink hat, tobacco-brown chiffon dress (tobacco was the newly fashionable color in 1939), two pearl necklaces, a pair of diamond clips, and

diamond ear clips. The dresses and hats are from Henri Bendel, and the jewelry is from Tiffany's.

77: Paramount Pictures actress Patricia Morison wearing an Elsa Schiaparelli-inspired Hattie Carnegie pink evening cape of rough caracul wool with a Tiffany necklace and Tiffany earrings. This photograph from *Harper's Bazaar*'s September 1940 issue was taken by Louise Dahl-Wolfe (1895–1989), who started photography in 1923 and began her career in fashion photography at *Harper's Bazaar* in 1936; Vreeland called her "passionate, ignited by her métier." The photograph is a composite: Dahl-Wolfe separately photographed the Metropolitan Museum of Art's ancient Egyptian mummy case of Khnumhotep. Patricia Morison's greatest success was the leading role in Cole Porter's 1948 Broadway musical *Kiss Me, Kate*.

78: Hoyningen-Huene's monumental photograph in *Harper's Bazaar*'s January 1939 issue shows a coral crêpe "sun-pleated" evening dress with a high, fitted waist from Jay-Thorpe, a Tiffany brooch composed of two diamond clips (priced at $22,200, it was included in Tiffany's display at the 1939–40 New York World's Fair), and a Tiffany diamond bracelet ($31,700).

79: Steichen's photograph in *Vogue*'s October 15, 1939, issue shows Gwili André wearing a turban by John-Frederics sporting the Tiffany brooch of two diamond clips also shown on page 78. The two-colored gold vanity case with lipstick was set with six rubies and forty-six diamonds; the bracelet had 606 diamonds weighing a total of 74.85 carats—Tiffany's priced it at $26,000. *Vogue* commented, "The fake can be fun, the synthetic can put up a nice show, but still eyes turn unswervingly to the real thing in jewels. . . . This may be the year of *Ersatz* in many things—but not in jewels."

80–81: *Harper's Bazaar*'s December 1939 issue included this two-page spread photographed by François Kollar (1904–1979), whose extraordinary 1931–34 work titled *La France travaille* included more than 10,000 photographs. Left: Elsa Schiaparelli's blue silk crêpe dress that could be pulled up at the waist to be worn in daytime. Right: Schiaparelli's short-sleeved black crêpe dress under a tunic jacket with a turquoise scarf and turquoise-lined tricorne hat. The center of the spread shows jewelry designed by Jean Schlumberger, a Schiaparelli protégé who was then serving in the French army. Schiaparelli (1890–1973) was born in Rome and spent her youth in New York City's Greenwich Village. In 1927

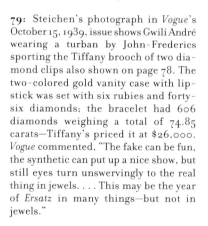

she began her career in Paris as a jewelry designer, and she had her first fashion success with butterfly-pattern sweaters hand-knit by Armenian women. At her peak she employed 350 seamstresses and the young Hubert de Givenchy. *Harper's Bazaar* fashion editor Diana Vreeland ran this spread to highlight Schlumberger's jewels at the center: she had made "Schiap" (as Vreeland called her) famous, and she was to make "Schlum" famous as well. He made the white sapphire, blue enamel, and diamond clip at center left for Mona Williams (see page 97), the pink enamel, diamond, and aquamarine bracelet at center for Mary Benjamin Rogers, the widow of a Standard Oil magnate, and the diamond bracelet at center right for the Scottish-born beauty Audrey Pleydell-Bouverie, whose previous husbands included department store heir Marshall Field. Schlumberger opened his first New York shop in 1946; he joined Tiffany & Co. in March 1956.

82: Wedding dress by Eugenie for Saks Fifth Avenue, a stiff white veil with a snood and satin bows, and a Tiffany flower spray of diamonds at the neckline with a matching bracelet. Photograph by Ruzzie Green for the Summer 1939 issue of *Brides' Magazine*.

82   83

83: A Hudson Bay sable coat from Stein and Blaine set off by Tiffany's American Deco "World's Fair" jewelry in Horst's photograph for *Vogue*'s December 15, 1939, issue.

84: A suite of stylized floral Tiffany jewelry photographed by Hoyningen-Huene for *Harper's Bazaar*, circa 1940. The matching earrings, necklace, ring, and bracelet are composed of pearls, diamonds, and gold; they are now in Tiffany & Co.'s Permanent Collection.

84   85

85: Tiffany's floral necklace and bracelet from *Harper's Bazaar*'s December 1939 (Christmas) issue. *Harper's* captioned Nordhausen's photograph, "She'll covet forever a slender vinelike necklace that follows so delicately the shape of her throat. The little flowers of amethyst quartz have a fragile quality not unlike the flowers of early spring. The leaves are dull green gold."

86: In this Steichen photograph in *Vogue*'s December 1, 1934, issue, the green crêpe dress and white fox cape are matched with emerald, pearl, and diamond jewelry from Tiffany & Co. The pearl sautoir was priced at $26,000, the emerald bracelet at $20,000, one diamond bracelet was priced at $17,500, and the other at $25,500, for a total

86   87

of $89,000—a fortune in the depths of the Great Depression. The dress was designed by Yvonne Carette, a Paris couturiere with a New York branch, and the cape was by Revillon, the leading Paris furrier who also had a New York branch. White fox was at the height of fashion in 1934, but two years later *Vogue* announced "a stampede for silver fox" (*Vogue*, December 15, 1936, p. 38).

87: Checked silk taffeta gilet and hat with field flowers by John-Frederics, photographed by Hoyningen-Huene with a 1903 floral still life by Pablo Picasso at the Jacques Seligman Gallery for *Harper's Bazaar*'s June 1940 issue.

88: Hoyningen-Huene's photograph for *Harper's Bazaar*'s December 1939 issue shows a Persian lamb coat and a cyclamen-colored felt hat by Suzy that *Harper's* called "[t]he completely appropriate hat to complete a black or dark blue outfit." With Tiffany's diamond button earrings and American Deco "spray-of-diamonds clip, like the flare of a rocket."

88   89

89. Jessie Franklin Turner's "mist-blue" pleated chiffon tea gown under a café-au-lait chiffon coat. In another Diana Vreeland "Why Don't You—" column, she suggested jeweled bracelets on one arm and all-gold bracelets on the other. Here, along with a Tiffany gold necklace (priced at $325), the model wears an emerald and sapphire bracelet ($1,375) and a ruby and diamond bracelet ($1,240) on her left arm, and two gold bracelets ($210 and $255) on her right arm. This photograph from *Harper's Bazaar*'s April 1938 issue was taken by Louise Dahl-Wolfe. The decor was by James Pendleton, a former Hollywood and Broadway dancer who had an interior design and antiques shop in New York. He moved to Los Angeles during World War II and became known as "the decorator to the stars."

90-91: Horst's two-page merry-go-round spread in *Vogue*'s September 1, 1940, issue. Left: a white caracal coat over a beige "Chanel-type" dress with a beige hat and Tiffany gold earrings and bracelet. Right: leopard collar and lapels—with matching Tiffany clips—on a black wool suit with a large leopard "muff-bag" and hat. Tiffany & Co. jewelry.

90   91

92: Toni Frissell's elaborately staged photograph in *Vogue*'s May 15, 1940, issue shows Jay-Thorpe's dove-gray silk marquisette dress and jacket with necklaces and bracelets from Tiffany's. Frissell began at *Vogue* as a caption writer in the early 1930s; this photograph shows the influence of Horst and George Platt Lynes. After World War II she photo-

92   93

graphed for *Life*, *Look*, and *Sports Illustrated*.

93: Horst's tableau for the November 15, 1940, issue of *Vogue*. The caption reads, "Brilliant and bejeweled and covered up is THIS winter's way to go to dinner and the theatre." Cap, snood, and dresses by Nettie Rosenstein and jewels by Tiffany. The model in red crêpe-de-chine wears ruby-and-diamond jewelry; the model in blue silk jersey wears a sapphire-and-diamond bracelet and earrings, and a sapphire-and-moonstone clip in her hair.

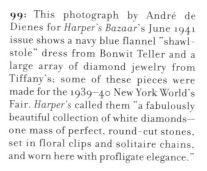

94   95

94: Left: Red jacket with Persian embroidery by Jo Copeland for Patullo and a necklace and earrings from Tiffany's. Right: Sada Saks's dinner dress of ice-green silk with ruby and rhinestone beads. Hoyningen-Huene shot this photograph for the September 1940 issue of *Harper's Bazaar*, which commented, "In deference to a troubled world, the new evening dresses cover you up. No matter how gay the party, you will have sleeves, a high back, a jacket—or all three. This is not modesty, this is fashion."

95: More medieval-revival hoods designed by Nettie Rosenstein, photographed by Hoyningen-Huene for *Harper's Bazaar*'s March 1940 issue. The model at left wears white chiffon; the model at right wears clinging white Celanese rayon jersey and a Tiffany necklace, bracelet, and ring.

96   97

96: A purple silk crêpe dinner dress by Germaine Monteil and Tiffany bracelets and ear clips in a Hoyningen-Huene photograph from *Harper's Bazaar*'s September 1940 issue. The lipstick is Germain Monteil's "Dark Fire," and the extravagant setting—with a cabbage-rose carpet, "Hollywood-baroque" mirror, and purple satin hassock—is by James Pendleton.

97: Cecil Beaton's hand-colored photograph of Mona Williams for *Vogue*'s February 1, 1938, issue. The daughter of a stable groom, she married her father's employer, then went on to marry multimillionaire Harrison Williams and became a celebrity: her clothes, jewelry, houses, and marriages were chronicled in the press for years. She was an early supporter of jewelry designer Jean Schlumberger: here she wears a magnificent necklace that Schlumberger made for her friend Daisy Fellowes, an heiress to the Singer Sewing Machine fortune and an even more extravagant society icon. Cecil Beaton had a long career as a photographer, illustrator, author, and designer; when this photograph was published, he was best known for his portraits of Queen Elizabeth (wife of

King George VI and mother of the present queen), and his Mona Williams portrait has a regal aspect.

98: *Vogue*'s December 15, 1941, issue featured Horst's photograph of Esmé O'Brien wearing a "half-hat" by Lilly Daché, hyacinth "ear muffs," and gold jewelry from Tiffany's. She came from a prominent New York family; four months after Horst took this photograph, she married Robert Sarnoff, son of David Sarnoff, founder of RCA and NBC. She later married John Hammond, a Vanderbilt heir and Columbia Records producer whose discoveries ranged from Bessie Smith, Count Basie, and Billie Holiday to Bob Dylan, Aretha Franklin, and Bruce Springsteen. Esmé Hammond's favorite designers were Mainbocher, Alix Grès, and Arnold Scaasi.

98   99

99: This photograph by André de Dienes for *Harper's Bazaar*'s June 1941 issue shows a navy blue flannel "shawl-stole" dress from Bonwit Teller and a large array of diamond jewelry from Tiffany's; some of these pieces were made for the 1939–40 New York World's Fair. *Harper's* called them "a fabulously beautiful collection of white diamonds—one mass of perfect, round-cut stones, set in floral clips and solitaire chains, and worn here with profligate elegance."

100: A couple at the theater photographed by Constantin Joffé for *Vogue*'s September 15, 1942, issue. She wears a Henri Bendel dinner dress, an Elizabeth Arden coiffure with Tiffany diamond leaves, as well as Tiffany's earrings, pendant necklace, two gold bracelets and an important Tiffany diamond bracelet.

100   101

101: *Vogue* captioned its December 15, 1940, cover, "Across the grey year of 1940—the familiar warmth of Christmas." The model wears a diamond necklace and American Deco earrings and bracelets from Tiffany's. Photographed by John Rawlings, who started his career as a prop builder in the Condé Nast photo studio in 1936 and went on to shoot fashions for *Vogue* and *Glamour* for thirty years.

102: Peruvian–Argentinian–New Yorker Señora de Barreda de Chopita wearing Suzanne Remy's velvet hat with a diamond-and-emerald clip from Tiffany's. Photographed by Horst for *Vogue*'s August 15, 1941, issue.

102   103

103: Debutante Alice Gwynne Allen in her costume for the Beaux Arts Ball, photographed by Horst for *Vogue*'s January 15, 1940, issue; the diamond-themed ball was held at the Ritz-Carlton Hotel in New York on January 26. According to

Vogue, her costume "was inspired by an old Italian print—a sleek, slender dress of silver lamé, a silver wig over her own blond hair, and—in keeping with year's motif—an armful of bracelets from Tiffany." Three years later she married Geoffrey Russell, a pilot in the Canadian air force; both came from prominent New York families.

104   105

104: Tiffany's 1950 Christmas catalogue shows a fashion model wearing a stupendous array of jewelry. The emerald-and-diamond earrings were priced at $6,900, the pearl necklace at $19,800, the emerald-and-diamond ring on her right hand at $18,600, the diamond ring on her left hand at $30,300, the diamond and emerald bracelets at $10,500 each, the vanity case at $1,000, the diamond watch at $7,400, and the emerald-and-diamond brooch at $39,000. This brooch contains the 75-carat emerald that Tiffany's had shown in a tiara at the 1939–40 New York World's Fair; the emerald was cut from a much larger stone in a belt buckle of Turkish Sultan Abd-ul-Hamid II. In 1949 Tiffany's reset the emerald in a brooch, surrounding it with 109 round and 20 baguette diamonds. In 1955 Tiffany's new owner Walter Hoving sold the brooch to his friend, publishing heiress Janet Annenberg Hooker. She gave it to the Smithsonian Institution's National Museum of Natural History in 1977. Today the museum displays this brooch in its Janet Annenberg Hooker Hall of Geology, Gems and Minerals.

105: Claire Powers wearing a short evening dress of nylon tulle and silk taffeta designed by Frank Starr and the emerald brooch shown on page 104 as a necklace pendant, photographed by Desmond Russell at the Carstairs Gallery for *Town & Country*'s April 1954 issue. Her husband, Augustin J. Powers, Jr., was an executive of the graphic arts company specializing in color reproduction founded by his father.

106: *Vogue*'s September 15, 1956, issue featured "sporting" furs worn in town, photographed on Park Avenue by Frances McLaughlin-Gill. Here the model wears "the perfect measure of lynx for city sheaths, the new three-quarter cut." The coat is by B. Wolman, the dress by Harmay, the turban by Emme, and the earrings and necklace by Tiffany's.

106   107

107: Black-and-white tweed suit with a black-dyed fox collar by Ben Zuckerman and a turban by Sally Victor with a gold-and-diamond clip by Jean Schlumberger. Photographed by Karen Radkai for the cover of *Vogue*'s October 1, 1956, issue.

108: In this Richard Avedon photograph for *Harper's Bazaar*'s December 1956 issue, Dovima (one of Avedon's favorite models) wears long Tiffany pendant ear clips and Mainbocher's fawn-colored crêpe evening dress with a close fitting bodice and a wide skirt. *Harper's* commented that the dress presents "a miraculous new kind of allure—revealing by [its] mysterious cut and cling to the best lines of a woman's figure."

109: Corduroy cape by Mainbocher and the "Four Leaves" sapphire-and-diamond clip by Jean Schlumberger, also photographed by Avedon for *Harper's Bazaar*'s December 1956 issue. *Harper's* commented, "The cape as Mainbocher sees it—buttoned (*not* wrapped) to hang quite straight from the shoulders to just past the fingertips. He sends it out on winter evenings in beige corduroy, lined with satin and interlined with wool. Beautiful beiges all: the cape itself, the lace-over-lamé dress and the suede gloves by André David."

110: Janet Beamish wearing a Tiffany diamond necklace and a three-tiered Norwegian blue fox stole, photographed by James Abbe, Jr., for *Town & Country*'s December 1956 issue. Her husband, Major Tufton Beamish, M.C., was a Conservative Member of Parliament.

111: John Rawlings's photograph for the cover of *Vogue*'s November 1, 1957, issue featured Revlon's "Red Caviar" lipstick and nail polish with Jean Schlumberger's 18-karat gold evening box and diamond ring and bracelet. *Vogue* commented, "One of the new ways to look at night: sparkling. White satin floor-length ball dress, sparked with crystals."

110   111

112: This extraordinary photograph by Karen Radkai from *Vogue*'s June 1957 issue shows platinum and 18-karat gold jewelry designed by Jean Schlumberger: his diamond "Cooper" bracelet, his sapphire and diamond "Morning Glory" earrings, and his sapphire and diamond "Sombrero" clip. Philip Hulitar designed the evening dress; *Vogue* commented, "Surprise without an ounce of shock to it: melon-yellow chiffon for summer evenings." Hulitar began his career as designer for Bergdorf Goodman in 1935; he opened his own business in 1949.

113: A spread titled "Beauty on the Gold Standard" in the October 1958 issue of *Harper's Bazaar* included James Galanos's dress of white butterflies on gold brocade. The diamond brooch near the waistline is by Jean Schlumberger, and the diamond pendant earrings are also from Tiffany. Photograph by Saul

Leiter, courtesy Howard Greenberg Gallery, NYC.

114: Straw hat by Sally Victor with diamond-and-pearl ear clips by Jean Schlumberger in Louis Faurer's photograph for *Harper's Bazaar*'s March 1959 issue. *Harper's* commented, "A large black straw, slip-covered in wonderfully out-size black and white polka dots of polished cotton. There is a high, turret crown bound in black silk grosgrain which makes for arresting balance."

115: Hat by Lilly Daché, coral earrings from Tiffany's, and a "greige" wool tweed dress with a short jacket by Larry Aldrich, the designer and art collector who established the Aldrich Museum of Contemporary Art in Ridgefield, Connecticut. Photographed by Richard Avedon for a feature entitled, "Blonde is the Thing: the Pale, Pale Colors," in *Harper's Bazaar*'s February 1959 issue.

116: Reversible charcoal and white wool coat and rust silk blouse with a cigarette holder, cigarette case, and ring from Tiffany's. A Vogue Pattern illustration photographed by Palumbo for *Vogue*'s August 15, 1959, issue.

117: Hannah Troy's white knitted wool suit and natural dark ranch mink coat, with Jean Schlumberger's clip and earrings from Tiffany & Co. Photographed by John Rawlings for *Vogue*'s August 1, 1959, issue.

118: The cover of *Vogue*'s December 1959 issue featured a white cashmere sweater with a cowl collar, and a diamond ring and diamond-and-ruby earrings by Jean Schlumberger. Photograph by Sante Forlano.

119: Richard Avedon photographed Sophia Loren wearing Revillon's massive blue fox scarf and muff with a ring and earrings by Jean Schlumberger for *Harper's Bazaar*'s July 1959 issue. Loren had her first starring role in *Aida* (1953); she won an Academy Award for her performance in *Two Women* (1961) and another Academy Award in 1991 for her "career rich with memorable performances that has added permanent luster to our art form."

120: Elizabeth Taylor's bare back displays a fortune in cultured pearls from Tiffany's in a photograph by Richard Avedon for the September 1960 issue of *Harper's Bazaar*, which described it as "a cape of pearls—epic in size, incredible in their creamy rose luster." Taylor had been voted "All American Best-Dressed Woman" by the Fashion Academy of New York in 1949.

121: In this memorable photograph, socialite, artist, and designer Gloria Vanderbilt posed for Avedon for *Harper's Bazaar*'s April 1960 issue wearing Mainbocher's gray Shantung evening dress with a gray-lined stole and Jean Schlumberger's "Ribbons" necklace. In its December 1959 issue, *Vogue* commented that Gloria Vanderbilt was "hopelessly (and quite happily) enmeshed in the Mainbocher *dharma*. 'To go there for a fitting is really like a ballet. The timing is so perfect, and there's this incredible economy of doing what is just to the point.'"

122: Jacqueline Kennedy in conversation with Alabama Senator John P. Sparkman at the luncheon following President John F. Kennedy's inauguration at the United States Capitol on January 20, 1961. She wears a beige wool crêpe overblouse-dress by Oleg Cassini, a beige felt pillbox hat by Halston, and a diamond-and-ruby berry clip by Jean Schlumberger. Her husband gave her the clip to celebrate the birth of their son, John F. Kennedy, Jr., on November 25, 1960. Photograph by Jacques Lowe.

123: Jane Fonda wearing Jean Schlumberger's 25-carat canary diamond ring in *Harper's Bazaar*'s September 1960 issue (the provocative "dress" is fabric pinned around her). The daughter of Henry Fonda, she was twenty-two when Richard Avedon shot this photograph and had just made her film debut with a leading role in *Tall Story*. Subsequently nominated for seven Academy Awards, she won for her roles in *Klute* (1971) and *Coming Home* (1978).

124 and cover:
Jean Schlumberger's "Jasmine" necklace, photographed by Hiro for the July 1963 issue of *Harper's Bazaar*. Diamond florets are suspended beneath large multicolored sapphires set in platinum and 18-karat gold. Born Yasuhiro Wakabayashi in China in 1930, Hiro emigrated from Japan to the United States in 1954 and became an assistant to Richard Avedon. Avedon introduced him to Alexey Brodovitch, and Hiro worked almost exclusively for *Harper's Bazaar* from 1958 to 1975. He remains the world's greatest still-life photographer.

125: Fiona von Thyssen-Bornemisza, third wife of billionaire art collector Baron Hans Heinrich von Thyssen-Bornemisza, wearing the "Plumes" necklace designed for her by Jean Schlumberger in 1960, here photographed by Henry Clarke for *Vogue*'s March 15, 1962, issue. The necklace is a stylized rendition of feathers composed of diamonds, sapphires, and rubies. Fiona Thyssen was considered one of the most beautiful women in the world.

126: Jean Schlumberger's "Coquillage" clip photographed by Hiro for *Harper's Bazaar*'s June 1959 issue. The caption reads, "A fantasy seashell of sapphires—round as reality—caught with gold fronds of diamonds set to reflect and fortify one another's brilliance."

126   127

127: Winking model with Jean Schlumberger's "Dauphin" (dolphin) clip between her teeth, photographed by Hiro for *Harper's Bazaar*'s December 1962 issue. This piece is often called the "Iguana" clip because Richard Burton gave one to Elizabeth Taylor: in *My Love Affair with Jewelry*, Taylor wrote, "Richard gave me this pin to wear for the [August 11, 1964] opening of *The Night of the Iguana*, which forever symbolized the early days of our marriage when we lived in Puerto Vallarta, while Richard was working on the Tennessee Williams film. To me, this is one of the most extravagant pieces that Schlumberger ever designed." Soon thereafter Burton gave her Schlumberger's "Orchid" clip: Taylor added, "Richard and I had a sentimental attachment to the Schlumberger iguana brooch because it symbolized when we were so madly, happily in love [and] he wanted me to have another memento by Schlumberger."

128: *Vogue*'s September 15, 1963, cover showed a "jockey cap" by Mr. John (based on hats by André Courrèges) with ear clips by Jean Schlumberger. The caption reads, "On both sides of the Atlantic, this light year, we'll be helmeted, casqued, domed—and off for high adventure in spectacular hats like this luminous space-queen oval of white satin, muffling the head with chin-strap, ear flaps, brisk visor. The coat, white-died Indian broadtail lamb, with a curving back. Coat by Maximilian." The photographer was David Bailey, a major figure in London's "swinging Sixties": the leading role in Michelangelo Antonioni's *Blowup* (1966) was based on his prominence as a photographer.

129: *Harper's Bazaar*'s September 1963 issue included this photograph by Melvin Sokolsky showing Tiffany's diamond-pavé platinum buttons on a jacket by Sarmi. *Harper's* commented, "An extravagant echo of the Twenties, a superb stroke of chic in 1963, tailors' buttons turned into extraordinary jewels." The Italian-born Count Ferdinando Sarmi worked for Elizabeth Arden from 1951 to 1959 and designed the gown that Pat Nixon wore to the 1957 Inaugural Ball. He opened his own New York ready-to-wear company in 1959 and won a Coty Award in 1960.

130: Jean Schlumberger's "Ribbon" diamond earrings and "Oiseau de Paradis" clip of yellow beryls, rubies, diamonds, amethysts, emeralds, sapphires, and aquamarines, photographed by Bert Stern for *Vogue*'s November 1963 issue. Bert Stern, a leading advertising and fashion photographer, produced and directed *Jazz on a Summer's Day*, an acclaimed documentary film about the 1958 Newport Jazz Festival.

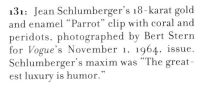

130   131

131: Jean Schlumberger's 18-karat gold and enamel "Parrot" clip with coral and peridots, photographed by Bert Stern for *Vogue*'s November 1, 1964, issue. Schlumberger's maxim was "The greatest luxury is humor."

132: Barbara "Babe" Paley wearing Jean Schlumberger's "Starfish" brooch on July 10, 1963. The second wife of CBS chieftain William S. Paley, she was considered the most elegant woman of her time. Photograph courtesy *Women's Wear Daily*.

132   133

133: Suzy Parker studying her makeup in an 18-karat gold compact by Jean Schlumberger wearing Schlumberger's 18-karat gold bracelet and a Russian sealskin coat and hat from Ritter Brothers. Parker was the first internationally famous model (the term "supermodel" had not yet been coined). In this Richard Avedon photograph for *Harper's Bazaar*'s September 1960 issue, her expression has a hint of wry humor that sets it apart from the stilted, "glamorous" poses assumed by other fashion models.

134: Coiffure by Monsieur Marc and a magnificent Jean Schlumberger necklace, photographed by James Moore for the April 1964 issue of *Harper's Bazaar*. The caption reads, "Diamonds, amethysts and rubies of incandescent, almost indescribable beauty formed a jeweled collar designed by Jean Schlumberger and fraught with romantic fantasy—bars of amethysts and diamonds, spaced by gold beads, and strewn with great round ruby and diamond flowers."

134   135

135: Blue linen jacket and sleeveless dress by Harry Frechtel with a hat by Halston and Jean Schlumberger's "Banana" earrings; James Moore's photograph in *Harper's Bazaar*'s April 1964 issue.

136: Donald Claflin's walrus brooch—based on Lewis Carroll's "The Walrus and the Carpenter"—has ivory tusks, a light blue enamel jacket with diamond-pavé collar and cuffs, dark blue enamel trousers, and a white enamel vest. Photographed by Saul Leiter for the December 1966 issue of *Harper's Bazaar*, which commented, "This precious assemblage is exuberantly young-in-heart, warm and laughing—from a store even older and more venerable than the Lewis Carroll verse." Claflin (1938–1979) had just come to Tiffany & Co. from David Webb.

136   137

128   129

137: The necklace with multiple strands of cultured pearls cinched together with bands of red *paillonné* enamel and 18-karat gold. Jean Schlumberger designed it in 1963, and photographer Helmut Newton placed it on the feet of a child sitting on a tiger skin in this photograph for *Vogue*'s October 1, 1964, issue. Newton was born in Berlin in 1920; at the age of sixteen he became an assistant to Yva, famous in Germany for her fashion, portrait, and nude photography. Newton moved to Paris in 1957 and soon began his triumphant career as a photographer of fashions, celebrities, and nudes. His often highly eroticized work has had a profound impact on photography, cinema, and video.

138: Jean Shrimpton, the leading model of the 1960s (Diana Vreeland called her "the Shrimp"), wearing Jean Schlumberger's pearl and diamond bracelet and clip, in an intimate pose with Steve McQueen photographed by Richard Avedon for *Harper's Bazaar*'s February 1965 issue. When Avedon shot this photograph, McQueen, a former U.S. Marine, had played leading roles in *The Magnificent Seven* (1960), *The Great Escape* (1963), and *The Cincinnati Kid* (1965); he later starred in *Bullitt* (1968), *Papillon* (1973), and *The Towering Inferno* (1974). The highest-paid actor of his time, he once told a reporter, "In my own mind, I'm not sure that acting is something that a grown man should be doing."

139: Silvered tweed top by Robert Sloan with a bracelet by Schlumberger, in a photograph by Bob Richardson for *Harper's Bazaar*'s December 1965 issue. Under the heading, "Christmas of Diamonds and Silver," *Harper's* described the bracelet as "Flower of diamonds. The blazing white fire of a broad bangle bracelet made of diamonds on gold, bursting into bloom with a full-blown diamond flower and two tiny buds—a precious bit of frozen spring to warm the heart of any girl." Richardson attended Alexey Brodovich's classes in the early 1960s and worked in Paris from 1964 to 1968.

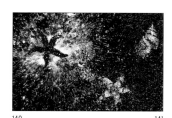

140-41: Hiro's Jackson Pollock-like photograph of Jean Schlumberger's starfish and conch clips for *Harper's Bazaar*'s January 1960 issue. *Harper's* captioned the photo, "Sea-trove: Schlumberger of Tiffany uses the precious jewels of the earth to recreate the fauna, rich and strange, of the underseas."

142: Model and actress Lauren Hutton wearing a black satin blouse by Lynn Stuart and Tiffany's coral bead necklace with a diamond-pavé, sapphire, and platinum owl by Donald Claflin. Lauren Hutton had just begun her career when Bert Stern took this photograph for the cover of *Vogue*'s November 15, 1966, issue, her first *Vogue* cover. *Vogue* reported seven years later, "'Like Holly Golightly, Lauren leads the life she wants,' said Eileen Ford, who took Lauren on in 1966 as a model at the Ford agency. 'Unlike Holly Golightly, her head is screwed on straight.' With the heroine of *Breakfast at Tiffany's*, Lauren shares something else: a breakfast-time at Tiffany's. When Lauren came out of Florida . . . she hit New York at 7:30 Sunday morning; and remembering little from a former fling at the city . . . she asked to be dropped at Fifty-seventh Street and Fifth Avenue. 'There I was, early Sunday morning, on an empty street corner with everything I owned—college test papers, old sneakers—in two suitcases, crying.'"

143: Vicountess Charles de Chezelles wearing Revillon's "Autumn Haze" brown mink double-breasted jacket and Jean Schlumberger's enamel and 18-karat gold "croisillions" bracelets photographed by Ira Mazer for the cover of *Town & Country*'s July 1966 issue. Hermine de Chezelles and her husband were French socialites living in New York.

144: Rayon and silk dress by Ginori with gold Tiffany bracelets, photographed by Bert Stern for *Vogue*'s April 1, 1967, issue. *Vogue* called it "a little brown dress with everything going for it."

145: Fuschia sleeveless long turtleneck sweater and cardigan by Pringle of Scotland. Donald Claflin based the gold, enamel, and jeweled brooch on Northwest Coast Native American totems. Photographed by William Silano for *Harper's Bazaar*'s December 1966 issue.

146: Princess Ira von Fürstenberg (actress, Fiat heiress, and a member of one of Europe's grandest families) posed for Gianni Penati for *Vogue*'s March 1968 issue wearing Donald Claflin's elaborately jeweled "Dragon" brooches suspended from a gold chain around her midriff. It was a daring pose at the time: Tiffany's Chairman Walter Hoving wrote *Vogue*'s Editor-in-Chief Diana Vreeland, "You certainly have discovered a new area on the feminine body where Tiffany jewelry may be worn. I must say I hope it ends there. If it goes much lower, I'm afraid they'll fire me off the vestry of St. Bartholomew's Church."

147: Donald Claflin's jade and gold bead bracelet with a diamond-pavé and gold Foo dog clasp (priced at $10,000), and his lapis lazuli bead bracelet with a diamond-pavé and gold dragon clasp ($9,700). Photographed by William Silano for the November 1967 issue of *Harper's Bazaar*; its caption commented, "Oriental fantasy in jewels—dog and dragon on the growl, making menacing faces as they run a glittering race across bare shoulders."

148

149

148: Aldo Cipullo's elaborate, oversized diamond-pavé and emerald earrings, photographed by Bert Stern for *Vogue*'s November 1967 issue. Cipullo, whose father was a costume jewelry manufacturer in Rome, came to New York in 1961 and worked for David Webb before joining Tiffany's in 1964. He later said, "Design has to be part of function. That's the secret of success. When you have function and design, married together, you always have a successful item." Cipullo designed these earrings to hold hair away from the face.

149: Brooch by Donald Claflin photographed by Hiro at Laurence Rockefeller's Little Dix Bay on Virgin Gorda for the April 1967 issue of *Harper's Bazaar's*. *Harper's* captioned it, "Coiled for action on a bracing nest of sea anemones, an underwater serpent of ferocious aspect—ruby eyes a-plot, diamond-spined emerald tail flicking dangerously—a challenging conquest for a collector."

150

151

150: Three multistrand necklaces of pearls, coral beads, and gold beads by Jean Schlumberger, photographed by James Moore for *Harper's Bazaar*'s April 1967 issue. The caption states, "Here, the precious, polished, billion-dollar look of today's affluent beauty."

151: Donald Claflin's pinwheel brooch with a central cluster of emeralds and diamond-pavé sails, worn by model Alexandra Afganisjew for Neal Barr's photograph in *Harper's Bazaar*'s November 1969 issue.

152

153

152: One of a series of diamond, coral, turquoise, enamel, and gold floral necklaces with detachable jewel-and-enamel beetle brooches designed by Donald Claflin in 1968. This photograph by Hiro appeared in *Harper's Bazaar*'s October 1968 issue.

153: Beaded necklaces and a turquoise, lapis lazuli, and coral brooch by Donald Claflin decorate this Salvatore Ferragamo—shod foot and ankle. From the June 1969 issue of *Harper's Bazaar*. Photograph by Ryszard Horowitz.

154

155

154: A sapphire ring and a ruby ring from Tiffany's in a 1993 composite photograph by Ryszard Horowitz for *Town & Country*.

155: Tiffany's vividly colored jewels of the late 1960s. Multicolored rings and a red python-skin bracelet with a detachable coral and gold mounting set with diamonds and cabochon emeralds, and another red python bracelet with a detachable mounting. Photograph by Gene Laurents for *Vogue*'s March 1, 1969, issue.

156: Justine Cushing wears a long white organdy dress with appliqué flowers designed by Donald Brooks, along with a large Tiffany cabochon emerald ring. Photographed by Frances McLaughlin-Gill for *Town & Country* in 1968 issue. The tall and striking Justine Cushing comes from a well-known Newport, Rhode Island, family that the *New York Times* called "a race of handsome giants." Donald Brooks started his career designing sportswear for Darbury in the mid-1950s, and he won the first of his three Coty Awards in 1958. He succeeded Claire McCardell at Townley in 1959 and opened his own company in 1965. He also designed costumes for forty Broadway and off-Broadway productions, nine movies, and seven television shows; his costumes were nominated for Academy Awards four times.

156

157

157: Halston's white evening dress embellished with Elsa Peretti's necklaces of single baroque pearls suspended from thin platinum chains. Photographed by Saul Leiter for *Harper's Bazaar*'s May 1975 issue. Halston, a successful milliner, began designing clothes for Bergdorf Goodman in 1966 and established his own company in 1972. His clean lines and solid colors set them apart from the exotica of the 1960s and the complexities of haute couture, and he was the dominant figure of American fashion in the 1970s. Halston included Peretti's earliest jewelry in his fashion shows and photograph shoots; Peretti later said, "I had this deep love affair with Halston without having a love affair. He was the pusher who made me successful."

158: Sophia Loren wearing Elsa Peretti's "Bone" cuff bracelet. The photographer is Francesco Scavullo, who began his career at *Seventeen*, then worked for *Town & Country*, and photographed hundreds of covers for *Cosmopolitan*, becoming one of the world's greatest photographers of fashion and celebrities.

158

159

159: Model and film star Raquel Welch wearing two gold Tiffany necklaces in this Bill King photograph for *Harper's Bazaar*'s October 1971 issue. The pendant of the lower necklace, designed by Tiffany's Sonia Younis, is set with emeralds and white and yellow diamonds centered by a cabochon sapphire. Raquel Welch became a sex symbol owing to the poster for *One Million Years BC* (1966) showing her in an aggressive pose wearing an animal-skin costume resembling a bikini. Years later she told an interviewer, "Americans have always had sex symbols. It's a time-honored tradition and I'm flattered to have been one. But it's hard to have a long, fruitful career once you've been stereotyped that way. That's why I'm proud to say I've endured."

160   161

160: Photograph from a spread titled "A Nostalgic Kind of Beauty" in the October 1971 issue of *Town & Country,* whose comment, "Hard-edged chic has gone by the wayside," turned out to be wishful thinking. Gunilla Bjorkman models a dress by George Stavropoulos; her tanzanite-and-diamond earrings are by Donald Claflin, as is the diamond necklace holding a butterfly pin centered by a tanzanite surrounded by white and yellow diamonds, with pear-shaped emeralds at the ends of the wings. Photograph by Francesco Scavullo.

161: Jean Schlumberger's "Ribbons" necklace and a dress by Yves Saint Laurent photographed by Barry Lategan for *Harper's Bazaar*'s December 1977 issue. The magazine called the necklace "a slim, flexible ribbon of gold, woven like a trellis so that it has depth and dimension. And liberally sprinkled with diamonds. To prove how nonchalantly you can handle all this splendor, run a ribbon through the necklace or tuck a flower in it." This necklace also appears on page 121.

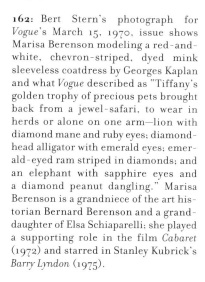

162   163

162: Bert Stern's photograph for *Vogue*'s March 15, 1970, issue shows Marisa Berenson modeling a red-and-white, chevron-striped, dyed mink sleeveless coatdress by Georges Kaplan and what *Vogue* described as "Tiffany's golden trophy of precious pets brought back from a jewel-safari, to wear in herds or alone on one arm—lion with diamond mane and ruby eyes; diamond-head alligator with emerald eyes; emerald-eyed ram striped in diamonds; and an elephant with sapphire eyes and a diamond peanut dangling." Marisa Berenson is a grandniece of the art historian Bernard Berenson and a granddaughter of Elsa Schiaparelli; she played a supporting role in the film *Cabaret* (1972) and starred in Stanley Kubrick's *Barry Lyndon* (1975).

163: Marisa Berenson in Hiro's "action-movie" cover for *Harper's Bazaar*'s May 1972 issue. Halston's Ultrasuede safari jacket is closed with an oversized, faux-ivory belt buckle by Elsa Peretti, who joined Tiffany & Co. in 1974.

164   165

164: Elsa Peretti wearing a Native American–inspired outfit by Stephen Burrows with her ivory "Bone" cuff and silver pendant and belt. Photograph by Charles Tracy. Burrows, the first African American to become a famous designer, opened a boutique called Stephen Burrows World at Henri Bendel in 1969.

Known for his narrow silhouettes and his use of irregularly cut, widely diverse fabrics, he won a Coty Award in 1977.

165: Elsa Peretti modeling her sterling silver "Bone" cuff with a silver lamé blouse and black leather pants by Stephen Burrows. Photograph by Charles Tracy.

166   167

166: Elsa Peretti with her King Charles spaniels wearing her "Heart" belt buckle and cuff bracelet. Photographed in 1976 by Francesco Scavullo.

167: Elsa Peretti wearing a slim beige dress by Halston with her ivory pendant necklaces and "Bone" silver cuff bracelet in the October 1971 issue of *New Woman*. Photograph by Chris von Wangenheim.

168   169

168–69: Elsa Peretti wearing an assortment of her necklace designs, photographed by Hilda Moray for the *Houston Chronicle*'s September 26, 1974, issue.

170: Pauline Trigère's Norwegian fox coat and red wool crêpe evening dress with a plunging neckline and flowing skirt, worn here with gold earrings and bracelets from Tiffany's. Photographed by Richard Avedon for the September 1973 issue of *Vogue,* which called the dress "clean, uncluttered, absolutely sensational." Trigère (1912–2002), the daughter of a Parisian tailor, came to New York in 1937, then joined Hattie Carnegie's staff. When Carnegie closed her design studios after the United States entered World War II, Trigère sold her jewels to establish her own business. Her aphorism, "When you feel blue, wear red," could be applied to this evening dress.

170   171

171: The model Justine with a coiffure designed by Vidal Sassoon and gold earrings by Don Berg of Tiffany's, photographed by Hiro for *Harper's Bazaar*'s August 1972 issue. Tiffany's introduced Don Berg's work in 1969 with a collection of diamond-pavé jewelry set with lapis lazuli and coral.

172: In 1976–78 New York fashion czar Ralph Lauren designed jewelry for Tiffany & Co. This photograph by Bob Stone from *Harper's Bazaar*'s April 1977 issue shows Lauren's coral plaid shirt under his safari-style dress with his gold and leather identification bracelet for Tiffany's.

172   173

173: Candice Bergen wearing Elsa Peretti's silver earrings and "Open Heart" necklace with a $20 pink Indian cotton shirt-jacket by Jeanne Campbell of Sportwhirl in Rico Puhlmann's photograph for *Harper's Bazaar*'s May 1975 cover. The daughter of ventriloquist-comedian Edgar Bergen, Candice Bergen made her film debut in *The Group* (1966), appeared in many other films, and won four Emmys for her title role in the television series *Murphy Brown* in the late 1980s.

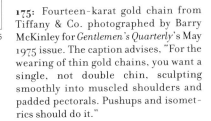

174: Two-piece rayon dress by Chester Weinberg, with Tiffany's gold earrings, bracelets, and cigarette case. Photographed by Chris von Wangenheim for *Vogue*'s February 1974 issue.

174   175

175: Fourteen-karat gold chain from Tiffany & Co. photographed by Barry McKinley for *Gentlemen's Quarterly*'s May 1975 issue. The caption advises, "For the wearing of thin gold chains, you want a single, not double chin, sculpting smoothly into muscled shoulders and padded pectorals. Pushups and isometrics should do it."

176: Jean Schlumberger's "Croisillons" enamel and 18-karat-gold bangle bracelets photographed by Jean-Loup Sieff for Paris *Vogue*'s May 1962 issue. Schlumberger revived the enameling technique called *paillonné* for these bracelets and several other pieces; its luminescence is achieved with several layers of enamel and gold jewelers' foil (*paillon* in French). These bracelets are often called "Jackie" bracelets because President John F. Kennedy gave a white-enamel example to Jacqueline Kennedy in 1962. She often wore it with matching "Banana" earrings by Schlumberger.

176   177

177: Patti Hansen modeling Angela Cummings's agate, jasper, and gold bead necklaces; black jade, jasper, and gold cuff bracelet, and gold bangle bracelets inlaid with jasper and lapis lazuli. Photographed by Stan Malinowski for the November 1977 issue of *Vogue*.

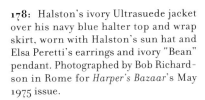

178: Halston's ivory Ultrasuede jacket over his navy blue halter top and wrap skirt, worn with Halston's sun hat and Elsa Peretti's earrings and ivory "Bean" pendant. Photographed by Bob Richardson in Rome for *Harper's Bazaar*'s May 1975 issue.

178   179

179: In one of Helmut Newton's most famous photographs, Elsa Peretti posed on the terrace of her New York apartment in 1976 wearing a mask, a Playboy bunny costume, and two of her necklaces for Tiffany's.

180: Elsa Peretti's gold wire earrings, diamond necklace, and heart pendant, worn with a Halston dress for the cover of *Newsweek*'s April 4, 1977, issue. Author Susan Cheever reported, "These days the crowds head for tiny lopsided hearts, gold and silver teardrops, lima-bean-shaped earrings, silver and ivory cuff bracelets and minuscule diamonds

dotted along delicate gold chains and sold 'by the yard' for necklaces. The landslide success of these unlikely pieces has sparked the most revolutionary changes in serious jewelry since the Renaissance. And oddly enough, it all began at staid old Tiffany's, with the arrival of a tempestuous Italian ex-model named Elsa Peretti." Photograph by Alberto Rizzo.

180   181

181: Elsa Peretti's carved rock crystal vases suspended from thin gold chains studded with diamonds. She based this early design on a bud vase suspended from a chain—intended for the back seat of a Rolls-Royce—that she found at a flea market. Photograph by Hiro.

182: Esmé modeling a low-cut dress by Stephen Burrows and Elsa Peretti's "Lobe" earrings and "Diamonds by the Yard" necklace, photographed by Francesco Scavullo for the cover of *Cosmopolitan*'s April 1980 issue.

182   183

183: Lisa Cummings modeling a dress by Fabrice, earrings by Jean Schlumberger, and a bracelet by Elsa Peretti, photographed by Francesco Scavullo for the cover of *Cosmopolitan*'s April 1981 issue.

184–85: Two pages from a six-page portfolio modeled by Kelley LeBrock and photographed by Stan Malinowski titled "Christmas at Tiffany's" in *Vogue*'s December 1980 issue. Shown here are necklaces and rings from Paloma Picasso's first Tiffany collection, introduced the previous month. The necklaces are made of quartz, rhodochrosite, charoite, jadeite, lapis lazuli, coral, and gold balls, many studded with small diamonds. *Vogue* commented, "Provocative wit. Positive. Daring in style. An unexpected bravado in jewels. Gold and diamonds used with positive abandon. Larger-than-life stones—beads the size of Ping-Pong balls. Flaming color. The start of something new, something big." In 1991 she told an interviewer, "Most people have to make a name for themselves. I had to make them forget mine. Forget the Picasso, build up the Paloma. Yet the only way to build up the Paloma is to admit that Picasso is part of it and not feel shy about it, even though the natural tendency is to feel guilt for something you don't deserve. Most people who have famous names don't even try because of that."

184   185

186–87: This spread from *Vogue*'s December 1980 issue shows Kelly LeBrock modelling jewelry and objects by Elsa Peretti. *Vogue* commented, "A sensuous simplicity. Revealed—in a unique way—the very elemental sensuality of precious stones and precious metals. Revealed in designs that become

186   187

instant trend setting classics: her diamonds-by-the-yard have sold, quite literally, by the mile. And now beyond jewelry, the play of sculptural, freeform shapes to touch, to use, to live with. . . ." Photograph by Stan Malinowski.

188: The famously beautiful Cristina Ferrare modeling a silver lamé cardigan by Zoran in *Harper's Bazaar*'s October 1981 issue. The diamond-pavé earrings and the multistrand platinum chain necklace with a matching diamond-pavé clasp are by Elsa Peretti. Photograph by Bill King.

189: Photograph by Victor Skrebneski for *Town & Country*'s August 1981 issue showing Jennifer Beals modeling jewelry designed by Jean Schlumberger. Tiffany and Co. celebrated the twenty-fifth anniversary of its association with Schlumberger at a retrospective in October 1981.

190: Brooke Shields wearing a shimmering black dress by Geoffrey Beene and a gold mesh necklace by Elsa Peretti, photographed by Guy Bourdin for Paris *Vogue*'s October 1982 issue. Shields achieved stardom at the age of thirteen for her role in *Pretty Baby* (1978); two years later she became internationally famous for her performance.

191: Hiro's photograph of a model wearing Elsa Peretti's sterling silver mesh earrings, and necklace, while holding Peretti's silver ring.

192: Isabella Rossellini wearing a pink satin dress with Paloma Picasso's jeweled rings and bracelet, photographed by Eric Boman in 1988. Daughter of the great Italian film director Roberto Rossellini and the great Swedish actress Ingrid Bergman, Isabella Rossellini worked as a journalist in Rome and New York before becoming the leading model of the 1980s. She also appeared in several films, notably *White Nights* with Mikhail Baryshnikov (1985) and David Lynch's *Blue Velvet* (1986). Of Swedish background and schooled as an artist, photographer Eric Boman worked in London and Paris before moving to New York in 1978. He is known for fashion, interior, and still-life work.

193: Isabella Rossellini wearing a plunging-neckline silk pantsuit by Thierry Mugler and oversized, freeform earrings by Angela Cummings, photographed for Paris *Vogue*'s May 1982 issue by Eric Boman.

194: Music critic John Canadry, whose essay titled "The Artful Body" accompanied Victor Skrebneski's photograph in *Town & Country*'s May 1982 issue, wrote that it depicted "Primitive woman,

dressed as she might have been before the dawn of history, in patterns of colored clays." The model wears Paloma Picasso's necklace with a diamond-pavé "egg." The intricate gold mesh chain is called a *chaine à l'impératrice*; its astonishingly complex design was developed for France's Empress Eugénie, who assembled one of history's greatest collection of jewels. The chain shown here was also made in Paris.

195: Important Tiffany sapphire and pear-shaped diamond necklace with matching ear clips photographed by Victor Skrebneski for *Town & Country*'s February 1983 issue.

196–97: Skrebneski's superb study of diamonds and feminine allure for *Town & Country*'s May 1983 issue. Abstract pink markings by celebrity fashion illustrator Joe Eula on a sheet of paper held across the model's shoulder highlight the drama of pear-shaped diamonds from the 1983 "Diamonds of Tiffany" collection.

198: Tiffany line necklaces and bracelets of square-cut diamonds and a ring set with a "starburst" diamond modeled by Kim Charlton. An important 26.54-carat emerald-cut diamond dangles at right. Another Skrebneski study of diamonds and feminine allure, for *Town & Country*'s August 1984 issue.

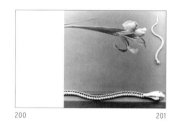

199: Paloma Picasso wearing her polygonal amethyst ring and aquamarine briolette earrings holding her multistrand seed-pearl necklace with an amethyst briollette pendant. Photograph by Bill King.

200–01: Elsa Peretti's sterling silver snake necklace and belt with an iris, photographed by Robert Mapplethorpe for *Vogue Italia*'s November 1984 issue. Fashion editor Nally Bellati wrote, "For ten years Elsa Peretti has been designing jewelry for Tiffany, and she remains at the height of fashion. Italian, ex-model, ex-interior designer, Elsa has conquered New York with the simplicity and cleanness of her design." Robert Mapplethorpe is famous for his more sensational photographs, but his still lifes are among his best works.

202: Supermodel Cindy Crawford wearing a swimsuit by Claude Montana and jewelry by Paloma Picasso, including an 18-karat gold and moonstone ring, an hexagonal palm citrine ring, and a cultured pearl and aquamarine bead choker with an 18-karat gold and calibré-cut diamond ball clasp. Photographed by Victor Skrebneski for *Town & Country*'s February 1985 issue.

203: Brooke Shields modeling a silver top by Stephen Burrows with Paloma Picasso's diamond-pavé earrings and gold bracelet studded with diamonds. Photograph by Francesco Scavullo.

204

205

204: The *Washington Post*'s Sunday magazine of November 23, 1986, included a fashion spread with a model posing as Frances Stevens, the heiress and would-be cat burglar played by Grace Kelly in Alfred Hitchcock's *To Catch a Thief* (1955). Here she wears a low-cut cocktail dress by Geoffrey Beene and Jean Schlumberger's clips, bracelet, and ring; the compact is also by Schlumberger. The caption reads, "8 P.M.—She's the soul of discretion in basic black and a shower of costly Schlumberger classics." Photograph by Andrea Blanch.

205: Paloma Picasso wearing her "X" necklace of multicolored gemstones, photographed by Kenro Izu in 1987.

206

207

206: An array of Elsa Peretti's creations in *Elle*'s December 1987 issue: lacquered hand-carved magnolia wood earrings, tasseled black silk choker with a silver clasp, lacquered hand-carved magnolia wood bangle bracelets, and a silk and bamboo handbag. *Elle* commented, "Streamlined, clean-lined, effortlessly elegant, worn clustered together or one at a time, these are your power pieces. Minimal fuss, maximal effect." Photograph by Tyen.

207: Elsa Peretti's gold-lacquered straw box, worn here as a pendant, with a white shirt by Michael Kors and a hat by Eric Javits. Photographed by Marc Hispard for *Elle*'s May 1988 issue.

208

209

208: This photograph by Sheila Metzner shows Michaela Berk modeling Elsa Peretti's sterling silver "Scorpion" necklace and "Bone" cuffs. *Vogue* quoted Peretti about the necklace, "I found the animal interesting in a mechanical way." Peretti said the cuffs were "the best things I've ever done. I believed in the design at the moment, and I still believe in it."

209: Supermodel Linda Evangelista wearing vintage denim cap, jacket, and jeans by Levi Strauss with a necklace and cuffs by Paloma Picasso. Photographed by Francesco Scavullo for the June 1990 issue of *Harper's Bazaar*.

210

211

210: Deborah Dickinson modeling a black cotton and Lycra one-piece bathing suit by Norma Kamali and Elsa Peretti's "Open Heart" pendant, from the January 10, 1982, issue of the *New York Times Magazine*. Photographed by Eva Sereny at Caneel Bay, St. John, Virgin Islands.

211: Bert Stern's photograph of supermodel Iman wearing an off-the-shoulder T-shirt with Elsa Peretti's sterling silver ball-point pen and "Flask" and "Open Heart" pendants, in German *Vogue*'s September 1988 issue.

212–3: Victor Skrebneski's photograph of Deborah Harris modeling Tiffany's diamond solitaire ring, diamond earrings, two diamond bracelets, and two ruby-and-diamond necklaces, one with 28 oval rubies and 212 marquise diamonds. Montenapoleone's silk lace red dress accentuates the rubies, and a photograph enlargement of Amedeo Modigliani's *Le Grand Nu* (1919) is in the background. *From Town & Country*'s February 1988 issue and *Harper's Bazaar*'s Paris edition for December 1988.

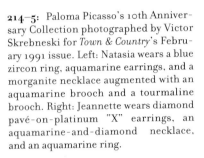

212

213

214–5: Paloma Picasso's 10th Anniversary Collection photographed by Victor Skrebneski for *Town & Country*'s February 1991 issue. Left: Natasia wears a blue zircon ring, aquamarine earrings, and a morganite necklace augmented with an aquamarine brooch and a tourmaline brooch. Right: Jeannette wears diamond pavé-on-platinum "X" earrings, an aquamarine-and-diamond necklace, and an aquamarine ring.

214

215

216: Elsa Peretti wearing her diamond stud earrings, photographed in her Rome apartment (decorated by the great Italian interior designer Renzo Mongiardino) overlooking the gardens of the Villa Borghese, from *Vanity Fair*'s September 1987 issue. Photograph by Gian Paolo Barbieri.

217: Elsa Peretti's gold snake necklace shown here with Louis Comfort Tiffany's circa 1910 iridescent Favrile glass vase, from *Vogue*'s December 1987 issue. Photograph by Sheila Metzner.

216

217

218–19: Paloma Picasso wearing her jewelry in "diva" poses for *Tatler* in 1991. Photographs by Albert Watson.

220: Circus acrobat wearing a hand-hammered 18-karat gold necklace from Paloma Picasso's "Maxi Boule" collection; photographed by Gian Paolo Barbieri for *Corriere della Sera*'s "Io Donna" of November 1997.

218

219

221: Flowing mousseline caftan by Adolfo, handbag by Judith Lieber, and Paloma Picasso's diamond-and-morganite ribbon necklace and pink tourmaline and diamond drop earrings. Photographed by Victor Skrebneski for Jeanine Larmoth's article entitled "Haute Couture American Style: The Free Spirit" in *Town & Country*'s May 1991 issue. Adolfo, born Adolfo Sardiña in Cuba, began his career as a milliner for Emme and opened his own New York

220

221

salon in 1962. He reached his zenith in the 1970s and 1980s with his full-scale ball gowns, slim evening dresses, and Chanel-style suits for day and evening.

222   223

222: Fitted satin top from Balenciaga, gloves with voluminous silk taffeta cuffs by Shaneen Huxham, a feather comb by Tracy Watts, and red enamel and 18-karat gold "Banana" ear clips by Jean Schlumberger. The model is styled to echo Jean Schlumberger's "Parrot-Bust" clip. From *Town & Country*'s February 1995 issue; photograph by Hans Gissinger.

223: Paloma Picasso wearing her polygonal amethyst ring and gold bracelet with a diamond-pavé clasp. Photograph by Bill King.

224   225

224: Elsa Peretti's sterling silver cuff bracelet enhances a romantic encounter photographed by Peter Beard for *Esquire Gentlemen*'s Spring-Summer 1993 issue. Beard is best-known for his photographs of African wildlife.

225: Elle MacPherson modeling Eva Chun's silk crêpe "tank" gown with a fur boa by Adrienne Landau and "Angel-skin" coral and diamond earrings by Paloma Picasso. Photographed by Rico Puhlmann for the March 1992 issue of *Harper's Bazaar*, which commented, "Pink versatility—as appropriate for an evening as a short day suit."

226: Gold-lamé leather suit by Yves Saint Laurent with Paloma Picasso's hand-hammered gold-link necklace, from the October 1991 issue of *Allure*. Saint Laurent once remarked, "Paloma Picasso is the perfect example of a certain elegance that consists of rigor and daring as well as a mixture of contemporary and classic elements of style. I admire her!" Photograph by Fabrizio Ferri.

226   227

227: Rachel Williams modeling satin jeans, satin shoes, and Elsa Peretti's sterling silver "Bone" cuff bracelet in a characteristically provocative David LaChapelle photograph for the February 1995 issue of *Details*. Early in his career LaChapelle photographed for *Interview* under Andy Warhol's tutelage. His more recent, drama-packed photos are often elaborately staged: one observer wrote, "Artifice underlies his every image."

228: Isabella Rossellini wearing a dress by Halston and gold-mesh earrings by Elsa Peretti, photographed by Francesco Scavullo for *Harper's Bazaar*'s July 1982 issue.

229: Black satin suit by Plein Sud and Elsa Peretti's snake necklace, photographed by Per Zennström for German *Elle*'s July 1995 issue.

228   229

230: Tamzin modeling Isaac Mizrahi's black shoulder-tie dress and Jean Schlumberger's aquamarine-and-diamond earrings and necklace. From *Town & Country*'s September 1998 issue. Photograph by Oberto Gili.

231: Francesco Scavullo's photograph for the cover of *Cosmopolitan*'s June 1993 issue shows supermodel Christy Turlington wearing a minidress by Lisa Bruce and pearl drop earrings by Elsa Peretti.

230   231

232: Black stretch-wool slip dress from TSE and Paloma Picasso's multistrand rock-crystal bead necklace. Photograph of Tatjana Patitz by Gilles Bensimon for *Elle*'s December 1995 issue.

233: Actress and model Andie MacDowell wearing a dress by Donna Karan and pendant hand-hammered 18-karat gold earrings from Paloma Picasso's "Maxi Boule" collection in *Madame Figaro*'s August 1996 issue. MacDowell's performance in *Sex, Lies, and Videotape* (1989) made her a star; she later appeared in *The Player* (1992), *Groundhog Day* (1993), and *Four Weddings and a Funeral* (1994). Photograph by George Holz.

232   233

234–35: Byblos cotton shirt over a Missoni sleeveless top with Paloma Picasso's earrings and Jean Schlumberger's "Croisillons" bracelet. From the February 2000 issue of *Jane*. Photograph by Jan Welters.

236: Cowboy hat from the J. J. Hat Center, red-lacquered pendant by Elsa Peretti, gloves by Hermès, and red-and-white stilettos by Manolo Blahnik. From *Harper's Bazaar*'s February 2001 issue. Photograph by Sølve Sundsbø.

234   235

237: This illustration of Elsa Peretti's lacquered, hand-carved magnolia-wood bangle bracelets appeared in Albert Watson's photograph for the January 1995 issue of *Vogue*, which captioned it, "RED ALERT. This year, accessories are seeing red. Bright patents, fiery lacquers, and rich leathers are covering all angles, from bags to shoes to jewelry."

238: Jacket, strapless bra, and pants by Giorgio Armani with a "Supermodel" diamond cross from Tiffany's. From *Harper's Bazaar*'s March 2002 issue. Photograph of Christy Turlington by Greg Kadel.

236   237

239: Karolina Kurkova modeling Gianfranco Ferrè's shirt and bikini bottom and Elsa Peretti's necklace with a Tahitian black pearl pendant and black silk tassel, from *Harper's Bazaar*'s March 2002 issue. Photograph by Patrick Demarchelier.

238   239

240

242

240: Gianni Versace's low-neckline jersey dress with Elsa Peretti's sterling silver "Scorpion" necklace, from German *Elle*'s April 2001 issue. Photograph by Phillip Dixon.

241: Elsa Peretti's 18-karat gold chain-mail bra photographed by Chris Craymer for *Madame Figaro*'s July 27, 2001, issue. Diana Vreeland once remarked about Peretti, "I think she could design a car. She could design anything very beautifully."

242: "Lace" triple-row diamond and platinum necklace adapted from a 1909 Louis Comfort Tiffany design. Modeled by Bekah Jenkins with a hat from Lacoste and a perforated Prada Sport top over Miu Miu's fuschia cotton T-shirt. Elsa Peretti's tiny platinum cross set with five diamonds hangs from a chain at lower right. From the June 2002 issue of *L'Officiel*, photograph by Karina Taïra.

243: The Spring 2002 fashion supplement to the *New York Times Magazine* included a portfolio by Jeff Riedel with English film actress Kate Beckinsale portraying Oona O'Neill (later Lady Charles Chaplin) photographed in the style of Hollywood glamour portraits of the early 1940s. Here she wears a dress

by Valentino and a pearl necklace and bracelet from Tiffany's. The caption reads, "Sitting pretty: when Charlie first laid eyes on the seventeen-year-old Oona, she was sitting alone by the fire at her friend Minna Wallace's home in Los Angeles. She was turned down for the part she had come to discuss with Chaplin, but she landed a husband."

244: *Harper's Bazaar*'s June 2001 issue included a portfolio by Patrick Demarchelier with models posing as Jacqueline Bouvier (later Kennedy, later Onassis) and her sister Lee. Here "Jacqueline" wears a silk dress by Emanuel Ungaro and four "Croisillons" (or "Jackie") bracelets by Jean Schlumberger. The caption reads, "Schlumberger bracelets became a Bouvier essential, but the siblings' classic evening elegance made them the toast of the East Coast."

245: English film star Kate Winslet wearing a tank top by Miguelina and Tiffany's sterling sliver "Round Tag" bracelet, from *Glamour*'s February 2002 issue. Winslet was nominated for Academy Awards for her performances in *Sense and Sensibility* (1995) and *Titanic* (1997). Photograph by Walter Chin.

244

245

Index

Photograph Credits

The author and publisher are grateful to the photographers
and magazines named in the List of Illustrations for providing the necessary photographs. Additional credits are
listed below.

Photograph courtesy of Kathryn Abbe: 110, 156

© Richard Avedon: 17, 108, 109, 115, 119, 121, 123, 133,
138, 170

© Neal Barr: 151

© Peter Beard / Art + Commerce Anthology: 224

© 1989 Center for Creative Photography, Arizona Board of
Regents: 77, 89

Photograph courtesy of Keith De Lellis Gallery: 2–3, 94

© Estate of Louis Faurer: 114

Courtesy of *Harper's Bazaar*: 239, 244

© Hiro: 124, 126, 127, 140–41, 149, 152, 163, 171, 181

© Ryszard Horowitz 2002: 153, 155

© Bill King / Collection of Janet McClelland: 159, 188,
199, 223

© Copyright The Estate of Robert
Mappelthorpe. Courtesy of Art + Commerce
Anthology: 200–201

© Joan Munkacsi, courtesy of Howard Greenberg Gallery,
NYC: 20

Paramount / Courtesy of Kobal: 24–25

© Elsa Peretti 2003: 181, 191

Reprinted with permission from *The Saturday Evening Post*
© 1953 (Renewed), BFL & MS, Inc. Indianapolis: 39

Photograph courtesy of Barbara Sieff and *Paris Vogue*: 176

Vogue © Conde Nast Publications Inc.: endpapers, 1, 5, 6,
10, 13, 29, 31, 35, 48, 50, 52, 53, 56, 57, 58, 59, 64, 68, 69,
73, 76, 79, 83, 85, 90–91, 92, 93, 97, 98, 100, 101, 102, 103,
106, 107, 111, 112, 116, 117, 118, 125, 128, 130, 131, 137, 142,
144, 146, 148, 155, 162, 175, 177

Photograph courtesy of Staley-Wise Gallery: 84

Acknowledgments

The author and Tiffany & Co. would first like to thank Michael Kowalski, chairman and chief executive officer of Tiffany & Co., for his confidence and his most generous, patient, and vital support during the evolution of *Tiffany in Fashion*.

We would like to give special recognition to: Eric Erickson, whose genius at tracking down the wealth of original film and print that illustrate this book brings such luster to the history of fashion photography; to Kay Olson Freeman, whose research into the careers of fashion designers, photographers, writers, and models sheds so much light on the progress of the fashion world and its American protagonists; and to Rollins Maxwell, whose enlightening captions bring such richness and texture to the history of fashion in America over the last seventy years. This is their book as well as the author's.

We are profoundly grateful to the legendary Eleanor Lambert, doyenne of fashion publicists and Tiffany & Co.'s publicist for more than two decades, for her friendship, patience, and essential guidance. Her unique perspective as the only primary source of seventy years of American fashion history is fundamental to *Tiffany in Fashion*.

We are also grateful to: James Galanos for offering his views from many decades experience as one of America's all-time great couturiers; to MaryAnn Aurora for calmly maintaining order in the trafficking of all the complex materials and personalities that went into the creation of this book; to Eric Himmel, editor-in-chief of Harry N. Abrams, Inc., for his generous support for both the concept of this book and all involved with its realizations; to Harriet Whelchel, our editor, for the enthusiasm, intelligence, and clarity of vision she brought to this project; to Ellen Nygaard Ford, our remarkable designer at Abrams, for the boldness and visual splendor of her compositions; and to Richard G. Gallin, our copy editor, for the focus he brought to the texts and captions.

The author owes eternal and heartfelt gratitude to both Charlotte Aillaud in Paris and Anna Piaggi in Milan, who introduced him to the worlds of French and Italian fashion more than forty years ago and so awakened a lifelong interest witnessed by this book. The author would also like to acknowledge Charlotte Aillaud's great friends Yves Saint Laurent and Pierre Bergé, who allowed the author to participate actively in the fashion world for the first time as manager of their fifth Saint Laurent–Rive Gauche shop, which was located at the Hotel Cipriani in Venice from 1966–1969; and to the late André Levi, director of production of Rive Gauche; as well as to Clara Saint, director of public relations of Rive Gauche; and Enzo Cicconi, former manager of the Hotel Cipriani and the author's business partner, for all their desperately needed help in seeing that that initial fashion marketing and retailing experience was a success.

Other members of the fashion world that contributed greatly to the author's understanding of fashion and deserve gratitude for their help include: Yves Saint Laurent, Pierre Cardin, Michael Fish, Thea Porter, the late Ken Scott, Vern Lambert, and Ossie Clark, who provided the author with extraordinary clothes during the 1960s; the late Carrie Donovan, for years of friendship and guidance through the intricacies of American fashion publicity; again Anna Piaggi, for teaching the author so much about fashion jewelry (or in her words to "say YES! to accessories"); and Tiffany's great fashion jewelry designers Elsa Peretti and Paloma Picasso, for bringing such style and quality and panache to Tiffany & Co.'s fashion jewelry collections.

We are very grateful for the exceptional help offered by: Nally Bellati; Sean Byrnes; Hiro; Staley·Wise Gallery; Norma Stevens; Michael Stier at Condé Nast Publications; Stéphane Houy-Towner of the library at the Costume Institute, The Metropolitan Museum of Art; and Michelle Zaquin, archivist at Paris *Vogue*.

The following were invaluable in providing illustration and advice and all deserve our profound gratitude for making this book possible: Kathryn Abbe; Vince Aletti; Noel Allum; Suzanne Aaron; Douglas Asch; Gian Paolo Barbieri; Neal Barr; Michael Berkowitz; Andrea Blanch; Steven Bluttal; Eric Boman; Barbara Bordnick; Center for Creative Photography, University of Arizona; Keith De Lellis Gallery; Gleb Derujinsky; Orlin Donaldson; Gert Elfering; Mark Faurer; David Ferber; Jessica Fields; John Froats; Michael Gallagher; Howard Greenberg Gallery; Michael Halsband; Ryszard Horowitz; Ronny Jaques; Dimitri Kasterine; Barry Lategan; David Leddick; Saul Leiter; George P. Lynes II; Stan Malinowski; Gwen Mazer; Janet McClelland; Sheila Metzner; Dennis Minkel; Jovanna Papadakis; Scott Park; Pat Peterson; Klaus and Anne Puhlmann; Alberto Rizzo; Charles Scheips; Eva Sereny; Barbara Sieff; Barbara Slifka; Sidney Stafford; Bert Stern; Michael Stout (Estate of Robert Mapplethorpe); Sølve Sundsbø; Charles Tracy; Charles Van Horn; Raissa Havrilak Vivona; and Elizabeth Watson. We would like to thank the following magazines for their contributions: Condé Nast Archive in New York; *Harper's Bazaar*; *Corriere della Sera*; *Cosmopolitan*; *Details*; *Elle*; *Esquire*; *Madame Figaro*; *The Saturday Evening Post*; *Tatler*; *Town & Country*; *Vanity Fair*; German, Italian, and Paris *Vogue*; and *Women's Wear Daily*, as well as the following photo and modeling agencies: Art + Commerce Anthology, Inc.; Artist Management, Inc.; Judy Casey, Inc.; CMG Worldwide; CMI; Creative Photographers, Inc.; Creative Exchange Agency; DNA Model Management; Elite; JGK, Inc.; i2i Photography; International Creative Management, Inc.; IMG; Karin Models; Kobal Picture Desk; Lighthouse Artists Management; Per Lundland; Management+Artists+Organization; Marek and Associates; Media 4; Julian Meijer Associates; Peters Fraser & Dunlop Group; PMK; Claire Powell, UK; Peter Safran of Brillstein-Gray; Luigi Salvioli, Milan; Rogers & Cowan; Stockland Martel; T Management; U Models, Inc.; United Talent Agency; Wolf-Kasteler; and Women Management, N.Y.

Project Manager: Harriet Whelchel
Editor: Richard G. Gallin
Designer: Ellen Nygaard Ford
Production Manager: Maria Pia Gramaglia

Library of Congress Cataloging-in-Publication Data

Loring, John.
 Tiffany in Fashion / by John Loring ; with essays by
Eleanor Lambert and James Galanos.
     p. cm.
Includes index.
 ISBN 0–8109–4637–8
 1. Fashion—United States—History—20th century. 2. Costume
jewelry—United States—History—20th century. 3. Tiffany and
Company.
4. Fashion photography—United States—History—20th century. 5.
Fashion—United States—History—20th century—Pictorial works. 6.
Costume jewelry—United States—History—20th century—Pictorial
works.
I. Lambert, Eleanor, 1903– II. Galanos, James, 1924– . III. Title.

TT504.4.L67 2003
391.7—dc21

                    2003004493

Printed and bound in Japan

10 9 8 7 6 5 4 3 2 1

Harry N. Abrams, Inc.
100 Fifth Avenue
New York, N.Y. 10011
www.abramsbooks.com

Abrams is a subsidiary of

 LA MARTINIÈRE
             G R O U P E

STEICHEN